A CLNICAL REVIEW ON PHYTOTHERAPY APPROACHES OF ACNE VULGARIS

A BOOK OF PHYTOCLINICAL

YASHRAJ YADAV

Copyright © Yashraj Yadav
All Rights Reserved.

A CLNICAL REVIEW ON PHYTOTHERAPY APPROACHES OF ACNE VULGARIS

By

Mr.Yashraj Yadav

Mr.Jeeko Basil Das

Mr Ashish Gupta

Mr.Anupam Mishra

Contents

Foreword

It is both a theoretical and practical field of study in clinical pharmacology. Backbone of reasonable and safe therapies. In contrast to the applied concerns of medical students and prescribing physicians, it is difficult to correctly and skilfully apply medications without a thorough knowledge of their basic pharmacology. That's why both basic background and clinical pharmacology are required in medical pharmacology. As part of the process of optimising drug therapy, researchers are collecting objective and quantitative data on drug use in humans, such as the relative efficacy and occurrence of side effects of various medications. Drug mechanism of action concepts are evolving. As a result, herbal medicines are being launched in a rapidly increasing number of countries. This suggests that having a tonne of information is critical. It is my sincere goal that this compact volume book will aid to remove medical students' fear of pharmacology and give prescribers with a brief and up-to-date source of knowledge on current concepts and breakthroughs in pharmaceuticals. Please accept my heartfelt appreciation to my colleagues who provided me with such insightful feedback.

Preface

Clinical pharmacologists have medical and scientific training that enables them to evaluate evidence and produce new data through well-designed studies.Clinical safety pharmacology combines fundamental, clinical, and pharmacotherapeutics. Concepts and priority medications change quickly. Innovation and progress are accelerating. Novel medications have been developed to target several new molecular targets. On the other hand, a large amount of evidence has been created to quantify the influence of various medications and regimens on well-defined therapeutic end objectives, therefore medicine is becoming more evidence-based. The latest edition emphasises evidence-based medicine by citing big randomised trials and other research that have impacted treatment practises. All chapters have been updated using the 'prototype drug safety' methodology and a structured, methodical, tabular manner. This version presents medication categorization as eye-catching infographics to aid remembering. Many figures, charts, tables, and highlight boxes The book ends with a list of relevant sources.

I thank my colleagues and students for providing valuable inputs and raising thoughtful queries.

As ever, the driving force behind this book has been Dr.GN Dherwheker and notionpress Publishers (P) Ltd, India. Cooperation and participation of my family has been pivotal.

yashraj yadav
June 2022

Acknowledgements

ACKNOWLEDGEMENT

The completion of this dissertation could not have been possible without the participation and assistance of so many people First of all I would like to express my sincere gratitude to my principal Dr. G.N Darwhekar, Acropolis Institute of Pharmaceutical Education and Research, Indore for his In valuable support and guidance throughout the progress of work. I would like to acknowledge my professor/guide Mr. Yashraj Yadav who counseled me with right idea sand provided his great deal of support and time for completion of my project.

I would be pleased to give my sincere thanks to all the faculty members who helped me consistently in defining the path of my research and shown the direction towards the successful accomplishment of my project.

Finally I would like to show my gratitude and thanks to my parents and friends from the bottom of my heart for holding up me consistently throughout the completion of my thesis work.

My sincere thanks to all

Regard

Mr.Yashraj Yadav ,Mr.Jeeko Basil Das ,Mr Ashish Gupta, Mr.Anupam Mishra

Prologue

A Clinical Review on Physical Therapy Approaches to Acne Vulgaris is a traditional clinical trial book. Rather, it catalogues in part the impact of clinical trials—particularly the randomised controlled trials on the practise of herbal medicine and allied fields—as well as the evolution and application of medical data and statistics. The latter has evolved in many ways through the direct needs of clinical studies and the consequent interaction of statistical and clinical disciplines. The impact of the results from clinical research, particularly the randomised controlled trial, on the practise of clinical medicine and other areas of health care and trament has been profound. In particular, they have provided the essential underpinning to evidence-based practise in many disciplines and are one of the key components for regulatory approval of new therapeutic approaches throughout the world. Probably the single most important contribution to the science of comparative clinical trials was the recognition, more than 50 years ago, that patients should be allocated to the options under consideration at random. This was the foundation for the science of clinical research and placed the herbal statistician at the centre of the process. Although the medical statistician may be at the centre, he or she is by no means alone. Indeed, the very nature of clinical trial research is multidisciplinary, so that a "team" effort is always needed from the concept stage, through design, conduct, monitoring, and reporting.

CHAPTER I

Introduction

Acne vulgaris is a chronic inflammatory disease of the pilosebaceous unit (comprising the hair follicle, hair shaft and sebaceous gland;) and is among the most common dermatological conditions worldwide, with an estimated 650 million people affected 1,2 . Acne is considered a chronic disease owing to its prolonged course, pattern of recurrence and relapse, and manifestations such as acute outbreaks or slow onset. Moreover, acne causes profound negative psychological and social effects on the quality of life of patients 3 .Acne vulgaris or simply known as acne is a human skin disease characterized by skin with scaly red skin (seborrhea), blackheads and whiteheads (comedones), pinheads (papules), large papules (nodules), pimples and scarring. Acne vulgaris is a disease of the pilosebaceous unit characterized by the formation of open and closed comedones, papules, pustules, nodules and cysts. Acne vulgaris is a common disease that has been associated with social isolation, employment difficulties, depression, and suicide4,7. The many treatments that are available indicate the dissatisfaction of patients and doctors with available therapies and difficulties in management of this disease. New, effective, and well tolerated treatments are needed. Early inflammatory acne lesions are characterised by the infiltration of the pilosebaceous duct with CD4+ T-helper-1 cells that are reactive to Propionibacterium acnes, a common cutaneous commensal.8,9 Colonisation of individuals with this bacterium is closely associated with the development of inflammatory acne, and the development of antibiotic resistance of P acnes is associated with treatment failure.10,11 The pathogenesis of acne is complex but dependent on four key factors including androgen mediated stimulation of sebaceous gland activity, follicular hyperkeratinization, colonization of the bacterium Propionibacterium acnes (an anaerobic bacterium as a normal constituent of the skin microbial flora), and inflammation 12. The high levels of sebum elicited by androgen cause proliferation of P. acnes in the pilosebaceous ducts and this proliferation triggers the host inflammatory response with a discharge of the proinflammatory cytokines, interleukin 1b (IL-1 b), IL-8, granulocyte–macrophage colony-stimulating factor (GM-CSF), tumor necrosis factor α (TNF-α) and complement deposition 13. In addition to P. acnes, as the main causative microorganism, Pityrosporum ovale and Staphylococcus epidermidis are present in acne lesions 14. There are 3 types of acne: comedonal, nodular, and papulopustular.Comedonal is non-inflammatory while nodular and papulopustular are the inflammatory types .15 Acne vulgaris is the most prevalent chronic skin disease in the United States, affecting nearly 50 million people.1 Acne is most common in adolescents and young adults but may persist into the 30s and 40s at a cost of $3 billion. Sequelae of acne include scarring, dyspigmentation, depression, anxiety, and low self-esteem. Specific estimates of prevalence for psychiatric comorbidities vary, and further study is needed.16,17 Acne vulgaris remains a common condition in industrialized societies, with many mainstream treatment options available. All these treatments carry risks, and none is completely satisfactory. Natural alternatives are gaining greater research support and have much to offer clinically. Antibiotic resistance in Propionibacterium acnes and Staphylococcus epidermidis has been rising steadily since the 1980s. In one analysis covering 10 years in the United Kingdom, carrying resistant bacteria were noted in more than 50 percent of patients who had acne and who were treated with antibiotics, with most patients carrying multiple different resistant strains on different parts of their bodies.18 Similar trends have been reported in many other industrialized nations.19 Despite some efforts by drug manufacturers to inform consumers, the incidence of women exposed to oral tretinoin, a known teratogen, during pregnancy has been increasing, possibly the result of direct-to-consumer drug advertising.20 These and other concerns, including cost, underscore the need for safer, effective, more inexpensive approaches, including those offered by herbal medicine. This article focuses primarily on herbal treatments for acne. Few botanical medicines have been evaluated systematically in clinical trials, and there is virtually no research on the common approach of natural-medicine practitioners for acne—recommending multiple lifestyle changes along with multiple natural products. Nonetheless, biologic plausibility has been demonstrated for many therapies in isolation.21 People with skin of color constitute the fastest growing segment of the US population,22 and acne vulgaris is a common cutaneous disease in this population. The relatively high prevalence of acne vulgaris in people with skin of color is supported by the literature throughout the past century. There are several published surveys on the prevalence of this disorder in blacks, Caucasians (whites) of European ancestry, Asians, and even Caucasians of Arab ancestry. The first of these surveys on acne prevalence in blacks and Caucasians was published by Fox in 190823 He determined that acne occurred in 7.4% (163/2200) of the Caucasian patients and in 4.6% (101/2200) of the black patients. In 1914, Hazen24 compared.dermatology outpatient visits for 2000 black patients with the visits of 2000 white patients. After diagnosing acne vulgaris in 8.4% of the black patients, compared with 9.0% of the white patients, he concluded that acne is almost as common among blacks as among whites. In 1965, Kennedy 25 Assessed the diagnoses of 3860 consecutive black patients from his private practice and compared these with 27,000 diagnoses of white patients assessed in another study. Kenney determined that 9.0% of his black patients were diagnosed with acne vulgaris, compared with 18.0% of the white patient population. Acne was the third most common dermatologic diagnosis in the black patient population and the most common diagnosis in the white patient population. Several more contemporary surveys have been published. Halder et al26 evaluated the diagnoses of 2000 black patients in his private practice and compared them with the diagnoses of 550 white patients. Acne vulgaris was the most common diagnosis in both groups, presenting in 27.7% of the black patients and in 29.5% of the white patients. In the United Kingdom, Child et al 27 recorded the diagnoses of 274 adult black patients and determined that acne vulgaris was the most common diagnosis, presenting in 13.7% of the patients. Child also compared the annual percentage of referrals for acne vulgaris in different ethnic groups and determined that 51% of the patients seen for acne vulgaris were black, 41% were white, and 8% were Asian or Arabic. Although prevalence surveys of Asian acne patients seeking treatment in the United States is unavailable, Goh and Akarapanth28 surveyed visits by 74,589 Asians (eg, Chinese, Malaysians, and Indians) in a Singapore clinic and determined that acne vulgaris was the second most common diagnosis, occurring in 10.9% of the adult patient population. Additionally, he reported that acne vulgaris was the 8th most common diagnosis in a pediatric population, occurring in 3.1%. Prevalence surveys of Middle Eastern Arab pediatric patients are also available. Though persons of this ethnicity are considered to be Caucasian, many also have skin of color. Nanda et al29did a survey of 10,000 Arab pediatric cases in Kuwait and found that acne vulgaris was the third most common diagnosis among preadolescent females (ages 10-12), occurring in 10.5% of the cases. In the United States, Schachner et al30 reviewed the visits of 2821 white and black pediatric patients and determined that acne vulgaris was the fourth most common diagnosis. Of a total of 142 cases, 49.3% occurred in black children and 50.7% occurred in white children. Thus, acne vulgaris is a common cutaneous disorder in individuals with skin of color, as evidenced by the fact that relatively large numbers of these patients seek dermatologic care for the condition. Prevalence data derived from private practice and clinic visits suggest that either acne occurs slightly less often in people with skin of color than in whites, or persons with skin of color seek medical services for this problem slightly less often than do whites. However, sufficient data from the general population do not exist to definitively determine the relative frequency of acne in people of skin color compared with whites. Undoubtedly, given the projected US population shifts, more people with skin of color with this condition will be coming to seek treatment from dermatologists. Thus, more information regarding prevalence, presentation, and special treatment concerns in this population is warranted.31

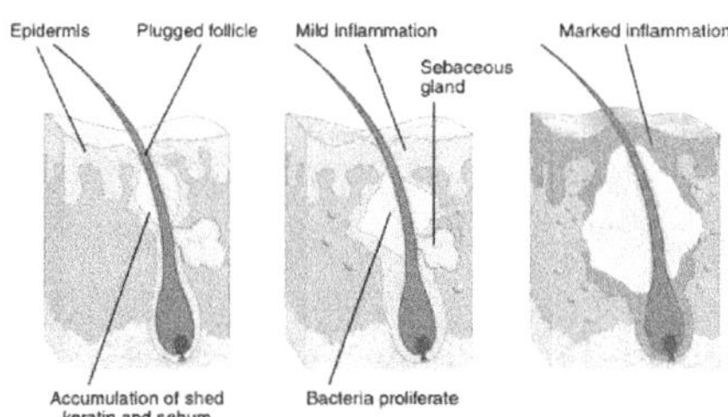

Acne vulgaris image with pathogensis

1.1 History of acne vulgaris

- Some degree of acne affects almost all people aged 15 to 17 years,11–13 and is moderate to severe in about 15–20%.32,33,34 Prevalence estimates are difficult to compare because definitions of acne and acne severity have differed so much between studies, and because estimates are confounded by the availability and use of acne treatments.35

- Surveys of self-reported acne have proven unreliable.36Although perceived as a teenage disease, acne often persists into adulthood.37,38 One population study in Germany found that 64% of those aged 20 to 29 years and 43% of those aged 30 to 39 years had visible acne.39 Another study of more than 2000 adults showed that 3% of men and 5% of women still had definite mild acne at the age of 40 to 49 years.40

- Acne typically starts in early puberty with increased facial grease production, and mid facial comedones8 followed by inflammatory lesions. Early-onset acne (before the age of 12 years) is usually more comedonal than inflammatory, possibly because such individuals have not yet begun to produce enough sebum to support large numbers of Propionibacterium acnes.41

- One prospective study of 133 children aged 5·5 to 12 years, followed up for an average of 2·5 years, found asynchronous facial sebum production initially, with increasing numbers of glands switching on sebum production over time.42

- Subsequent expansion of the propionibacterium skin flora (in the nares and then facial skin) occurred earlier in children who developed acne than in children of the same age and pubertal status who did not, suggesting that postponement of sebum production or expansion of propionibacterium skin flora until after puberty could prevent acne or minimise disease severity. Predictors of acne severity include early onset of comedonal acne,8 and increasing number of family members with acne history. Factors that can cause acne to flare include the menstrual cycle, picking, and emotional stress 43,44

- Beliefs about external factors affecting acne vary according to ethnic group45 Acne vulgaris is a chronic disease that often persists for many years.46 There is little research about what factors might predict whether acne will last into adulthood.47

- We could not find any good quality cohort studies summarising the natural history of acne. Sequential prevalence surveys of diff erent populations showing a gradual decrease in acne prevalence after the age of 20 years weakly underpin our current understanding of the natural history of acne. Mild inflammatory acne declines or disappears in a large proportion of those with acne in their teens. Cytokines that induce comedogenic changes at the follicular infundibulum might also inhibit lipid secretion from the sebaceous gland, resulting in remission of individual lesions.48 However, seborrhoea persists throughout adult life, long after inflammatory lesions have resolved.49Adult acne related to circulating androgens goes by several names, including post-adolescent or late-onset acne, and occurs most commonly in women beyond the age of 25 years.50 .2 How common is acne. A degree of acne affects nearly all people between the ages of 15 and 17 years11–13 and in 15–20% of young people, acne is moderate to severe.51,52,53 Prevalence rates of acne by age,51,52,53,54,55and 1996 census data estimated that 40–50 million U.S. individuals have acne, with an 85% prevalence rate in those aged 12–24 years.56 A study by Lucky et al.57found that the severity of acne in boys correlated with pubertal maturation and that 50% of 10- and 11- year-old boys had more than 10 comedones. Another study by the same team showed that 78% of girls between aged 8 and 12 years had acne.58 Of note, the severity of acne increased with advancing maturity and prepubertal girls with severe acne had notably higher dehydroepiandrosterone sulphate levels 59,60 Acne consistently represents the top three most prevalent skin conditions in the general population as found in large studies in the U.K., France and the U.S.A.61,62 Duration of acne. Acne begins in the early teens with the onset of facial sebum production and facial comedones followed by inflammatory lesions.54,63 Acne can occur in prepubertal children but this is usually non inflammatory in nature as children have not yet begun production of sebum, which provides the correct environment to host P. acnes. 64 Around 20% of neonates have an acneiform eruption but this usually resolves by 3 months.65 One Danish study has shown that the average age at onset of puberty in boys has dropped from 11Æ92 to 11Æ66 years over a 15-year period.66 postulated that this younger age of puberty was the reason for the observation that younger patients between the ages of 8 and 11 were presenting with acne in their clinics. Acne is a chronic disease and can persist, in some cases, into adulthood,67,68,69for unclear reasons.70A German population study found 64% of those aged 20–29 years and 43% of those between 30 and 39 years had visible acne71 And another study of 2000 adults found that 3% of men and 5% of women still had a degree of acne between the ages of 40 and 49.72 Sequential prevalence studies showing that acne decreases with age are not as strong as cohort studies that document natural history of acne over time in the same individuals. Self-reported acne studies are unreliable.73 We found few high-quality cohort studies of acne, which may be because studies of this nature are often difficult to conduct particularly due to the widespread availability of acne therapy additionally, the definition of acne and its severity has varied so much over time that it is difficult to compare and collate the results of different studies. Page 8 outcome measure needs to be employed for future studies.10 Predictors of acne severity include family members with acne and the early onset of comedonal acne 54,74 Longitudinal studies in the natural history of acne are required, in particular with a view to identifying risk factors for severe disease. It is unknown whether or not prepubertal treatment can alter P. acnes colonization and therefore subsequent inflammatory acne. Acne vulgaris and its association with self-consciousness, anxiety in social interaction, dissatisfaction with appearance and overall impaired quality of life is well reported.51 , 75,76 A recent review of studies by Dunn et al.77 concluded that acne can negatively affect quality of life, self-esteem and mood, and increase the risk of anxiety, depression and suicidal ideation. Female subjects score worse than males in the Dermatology Life Quality Index and acne quality of life self-assessment score, and impact upon quality of life is associated with longer acne duration.78,79,80 Depression and anxiety are often seen more in female subjects.80-83 The media's portrayal of flawless skin as an ideal is in part a culprit of psychological morbidity in females.84 Halvorsen.85 in a well-conducted questionnaire-based cross-sectional survey found suicidal ideation and substantial acne to have a threefold increase compared with mild acne in male subjects. Magin et al.86On the other hand, in a prospective cohort study in 244 subjects, found no correlation between acne and acne severity and psychological or psychiatric morbidity, although the study would have benefited from longer follow-up. An association with low attachment to friends and not thriving at school has also been noted.85 Quality of life does not always correlate with acne severity,87,88 Although some surveys have noted a correlation.89,90The presence of acne lowers the perception of overall health,91 and teasing and bullying is also a significant cause of morbidity.92 This article seeks to provide a comprehensive review on the epidemiology of acne vulgaris. The epidemiology of other forms of acne – acne rosacea, infantile acne and acne inversa (hidradenitis suppurativa) – are not discussed in this review. 93-95We begin with an overview of the descriptive epidemiology of acne vulgaris including incidence, prevalence, severity, morbidity, economics and financial implications, demographics and natural history 1.3 Epidemiology of acne vulgaris The Global Burden of Disease Study 2010 found that acne vulgaris (henceforth acne) is the eight most common skin disease, with an estimated global prevalence (for all ages) of 9.38%96 . In different countries and among different age groups, the prevalence of acne varies, with estimates ranging from 35% to close to 100% of adolescents having acne at some point97 .Acne vulgaris" in combination with epidemiology, adolescence, puberty, genetics, race, nationality, socioeconomic status, diet, Western diet, dairy, whey protein, chocolate, glycemic index, drugs, smoking, nicotine, oral contraceptives, and treatment. All review articles published within the last decade that included the previously mentioned terms were examined in addition to the articles which they cited that contained one or more of the previous key search terms in their title. Articles that focused on a population outside of the adolescent to young adult period were excluded in this study. Analysis of burden of the disease of acne vulgaris was done using the data from the GBD Compare search software98Globally, epidemiological studies have demonstrated a higher incidence of acne vulgaris in different ethnicities of color in samples collected from the population aged 10–70.years.99,100However, contradictory evidence exists as to whether a biological difference actually exists among various racial or ethnic groups in the pathogenesis of acne.101,102 Moreover, there are no reported studies that delineate the incidences of acne vulgaris among these different ethnicities in patients who are in their late adolescence. To address this, we analyzed the collection of data gathered from the 2010 GBD. Compare study over specific regions, controlling for specific age ranges (in this case, 15–19- year olds) to see the trend in disability-adjusted life year (DALY) rates per 100,000 people. The DALY rate is equal to the years of life lost plus the years living with the disability (YLDs).

Since the years of life lost for acne vulgaris is zero, the rate of DALYs is equal to the rate of YLDs. Calculation of YLDs is defined as the prevalence of the disease multiplied by the relevant disability weight. By dividing the rate of DALYs of 15–19-year olds by the rate of DALYs of all ages within the given population, we are left with a surrogate measure of the comparative rate of incidences of acne vulgaris in people aged 15–19 years per 100,000 people in any region listed between 1990 and 2010.There is an abundance of epidemiological research done in the US and other "first world" countries documenting an increased prevalence of patients with skin of color being seen for acne vulgaris.[104] While the pathogenesis of acne has not been shown to differ biologically between those with light skin versus dark skin, the difference in post inflammatory hyperpigmentation has been well established and is often the main concern regarding acne in patients with skin of color.[105,106] Coupled with an enhanced access to health care, it is no wonder why the US and other first world regions would report higher incidences of acne in dark-skinned individuals. At least in the US, as the Affordable Care Act continues to enhance the health care access in our society and as the projected US population continues to shift, these reported incidences within different ethnic groups will undoubtedly continue to increase.As noted, cultural perceptions or attitudes toward acne are also reflected in our analysis. For example, it has been noted that the South Asian population, in general, tend to believe that diet and poor hygiene play a significant role in the pathogenesis of acne and tend to self-treat by excessive scrubbing or face washing.[106] This common perception was addressed in 2005 by a comprehensive systematic review of eleven studies which concluded that there was insufficient evidence to link facial cleansing or hygiene maintenance to causing, exacerbating, or curing acne vulgaris in patients.[107,108]

The incidence of acne vulgaris in this population is complicated by poor access to health care and a cultural belief in holistic and complementary medicine.[106] Taken as a whole, this population is less likely to take oral medications or consult a licensed dermatologist or physician.Cultural differences regarding skin and hair care practices have also been cited as possible factors contributing to the variable incidence of acne vulgaris among different ethnic populations. Within the black population, for example, a common practice is frequent use of lotions containing cocoa butter, a highly comedogenic substance, with the intent to get even skin tone and improve hyperpigmented scars .[106]

Other reports have described patients of African descent using certain pomades (a mixture of petrolatum, lanolin, and oils) as a moisturizer for their hair and scalp, with acne erupting secondary to long-term use.[109]

Etiology and Pathophysiology of Acne

A number of pathophysiologic factors contribute to the development of acne, beginning with increased prepubertal androgen production, followed in a generally sequential manner by abnormal pilosebaceous follicular keratinization and desquamation; increased proliferation of sebocytes, enlarged sebaceous glands, and augmented secretion of sebum; obstruction of sebaceous follicles; colonization of pilosebaceous units by Propionibacterium acnes; and perifollicular inflammation.[110] Follicular hyperkeratinization, sebocytic hyperplasia, and seborrhea are all dependent on androgens.[111,113]

Factors that can lead to acne are as follows: SG produces more sebum, hypercornification of the sebaceous ducts, colonization of Propionibacterium acnes in the pilosebaceous ducts and inflammation. Severity of acne is connected with seborrhea which is associated with follicular infundibulum. In case of milder acne, there occur hypercornification, hyperkeratinization, and hypo desquamation of keratinocytes of the infundibulum which lead to the production of comedones. In severe acne, infundibulum breaks and releases sebum into the dermis which produces inflammatory responses.

- Increased Androgen production in sebum

As far production of sebum in the body is concerned, it is produced by the sebocytes dissolution in sebaceous lobules then they are passed to the follicle via sebaceous ducts, and finally, reach to skin surface by means of infundibulum. SG is mainly found in face and truck, i.e., the regions where acne generally forms [114,115,116]. After the onset of puberty androgen, production increases within the body and SG are the main target organ for the same because they have higher androgen receptors in skin [117,118]. Testosterone is the main androgen responsible for acne. One of its derivatives is dihydrotestosterone formed in the body by the action of enzyme 5α-reductase (type-1).

Type-1 of 5α- reductase is the foremost isotype found in human skin, specifically in the SG rich area [119-122]. As sebum content rises in acne patients due to rising androgen levels and also regulated by them[123].

- Metabolism of androgens in seabocytes

Sebum production is mainly regulated by dehydroepiandrosterone sulfate (DHEA-S). This androgen has highest sebum concentration and is present in an equal amount in both male and females. DHEA-S is considered as weak androgen, but the sebocytes have required enzymes to convert it into strong androgens (androstenedione, testosterone, and dihydrotestosterone). Despite their formation within the sebocytes, these androgens can also be re-up taken by the sebocytes. After the reuptake, testosterone and dihydrotestosterone bind to the receptor of cytoplasmic androgen to form a complex of androgen and receptor which enters the nucleus via nucleopore and binds to specific gene sequences in the nucleus [124].

Seborrhea

With few exceptions ("free" sebaceous glands in the genital region and mucosa of the cheek), sebaceous glands are associated with hair follicles. Sebum is formed by dissolution of sebocytes in the sebaceous lobules (holocrine secretion), transported to the follicle by a draining sebaceous duct and reaches the skin surface via the infundibulum.

The largest sebaceous glands are found on the face and upper trunk, i.e. regions where acne preferentially occurs. Large conglomerations of sebaceous glands associated with fine hairs are characteristic for sebaceous follicles. It has been long known that sebum production in the sebocytes is regulated by androgens. Acne patients generally display increased sebum production (seborrhea). Eunuchs produce less sebum due to androgen deficiency and do not develop acne.

Androgens, sebum production and acne are closely associated at certain ages. In the first months of life temporarily increased androgen production leads to excess sebum and occasionally to acne of the newborn (acne neonatorum). After regression of early androgen production, little sebum is produced in childhood and acne is almost never observed. At an age of 8–10 years, the adrenal glands and later the gonads start producing androgens. This results in enlargement of the sebaceous glands, increased sebum production and acne in teenagers.

The main sources of androgens are the adrenal glands and gonads, even though the skin itself is capable of synthesizing androgens. Androgens reach their target organs via the bloodstream, affect gender differentiation, and promote musculoskeletal growth. In the skin they stimulate sebum production in sebocytes. This results in an increased proliferation of sebaceous glands and increased sebum production; the responsible genes have not yet been identified. In sebocyte cultures, testosterone and dihydrotestosterone stimulate cell proliferation and lipid synthesis, to a higher degree in sebocytes from the face than in those from the legs [125].

Follicular hyperkeratosis

A further prerequisite for developing acne is a disturbed follicular keratinization leading to hyperkeratosis. In normal hair follicles, keratinocytes are loosely layered. They are regularly desquamated and carried by sebum flow to the skin surface.There is a balance between newly produced and desquamated cells. In contrast, in follicles affected by acne there is an increased keratinocyte proliferation rate, the densely packed horny lamellae do not desquamate properly and are not transported by sebum to the skin surface . A retention-proliferation hyperkeratosis results, first as a nonvisible microcomedo and finally as a comedo. Several factors are held responsible for the follicular hyperkeratosis. These include changes in the lipid composition of sebum, bacterial metabolites and mediators of inflammation. One theory is based on the assumption that keratinocytes of the hair follicle are supplied with linoleic acid via the sebum. Increased sebum flow in the face of a constant supply of linoleic acid results in a decreased linoleic acid concentration in sebum and thus a relative follicular deficiency in linoleic acid.Overall linoleic acid deficiency, such as in malnutrition, results in a generalized hyperkeratosis of exposed skin. In analogy, follicular hyperkeratosis in acne can be viewed as a localized, follicular linoleic acid deficiency. Comedogenic sebum components serve as a further explanation. These include fatty acid peroxides and squalene peroxide, which is formed by UV-irradiation of the sebum lipid squalene. Comedogenic effects of androgens have been suspected, because antiandrogens reduced comedogenesis independent of sebum production in certain individuals. Recently, the body's own inflammatory mediators have stirred scientific interest as a possible comedogenic substance. It has been shown experimentally that the presence of a certain concentration of interleukin-1 is sufficient to produce follicular hyperkeratosis in a normal hair follicle.[126]

- Linoleic acid deficiency

Linoleic acid plays an important role in the creation of intracellular lipid lamellae after incorporation with sphingolipids in follicular epithelium. Linoleic acid deficiency is very important in the etiology of acne as such condition causes impairment in the follicular epithelium barrier which allows the other free fatty acids produced by bacterial lipase activity or/ and by the metabolism of sebocytes to enter the epithelium and cause localized deficiency of essential lipids. Zouboulis showed that linoleic acid can regulate the interleukin (IL)-8 secretions and thus regulate the inflammatory responses [127,128]

- Microbial colonization

Propionibacterium acnes is a pleomorphic diphtheroid rod and belongs to the resident flora of human skin. Propionibacteria are the dominant bacteria in hair follicles; they prefer microaerophilic or anaerobic conditions and preferentially colonize regions with high sebum production. Seborrhea and simultaneous follicular hyperkeratosis obviously promote proliferation of propionibacteria.

A four log higher concentration of propionibacteria is found in 11- to 20-year-olds with acne in comparison to the similarly aged without acne.

The role of propionibacteria in acne is due to strong proliferation with resulting increase in bacterial metabolites which have a proinflammatory action. Bacterial lipases were suspected first, as they release fatty acids from esters. Free fatty acids above a certain concentration are irritative and proinflammatory.Later other potentially proinflammatory bacterial metabolites were identified such as proteases, hyaluronidases and chemotactic factors that can attract neutrophils and cause an inflammatory infiltrate in the follicular wall and in the surrounding dermis. When neutrophils enter a follicle and phagocytize propionibacteria, hydrolytic substances are released and further promote the inflammatory reaction. Propionibacteria are bound by the surface receptor TLR-2 (toll-like receptor 2). This binding induces monocytic cells, among others, to produce the inflammatory mediator interleukin-8, which chemotactically attracts neutrophils129.Propionibacteria activate the classical and alternative complement pathways. Besides these stimulating effects on the innate, nonspecific immune system, interactions with the adaptive, antigen-specific immune system occur.

Immunological factors and inflammation

Immunological and inflammatory factors influence the development and course of acne in various ways. For a long time, inflammation was viewed only as a result of the three other pathogenetic factors, especially bacterial metabolites. New data show that acne patients possess a tendency to follicular inflammation from the outset . It is presumed that leukocytes surrounding the follicle, especially helper T lymphocytes, initiate comedones by production of cytokines such as IL-1 and thus pave the way for acne development. Inflammatory processes can also increase sebum production. The inflammatory mediator leukotriene B4 binds to a receptor on sebocytes, peroxisome proliferator-activated receptor-! which regulates lipid metabolism. This relationship is supported by the observation that the leukotriene antagonist zileuton leads to decline in sebum lipids [130].

- Genetic factors

Predisposition of acne can also occur genetically. Very little knowledge is obtained about the hereditary mechanisms. Numerous genes are responsible for it. Among them, the main are cyt-P450-1A1 and steroid 21-hydrolase which controls adrenal glands androgen production. People having XYY karyotype show a severe type of acne [13]

- Oxygen stress and free radicals

One of the hypotheses also said that in response to the invading microorganism the phagocytes of the body such as neutrophils release reactive oxygen species (ROS) to cause lysis of the invading cell. These ROS are involved in inflammation[132]

1. Types and grading of acne

Although acne vulgaris has plagued humankind since antiquity, the need for grading acne vulgaris was felt when the therapies available for treating acne increased in the 1950s. Probably, the first person to use a scoring system for acne vulgaris was Carmen Thomas of Philadelphia.

She used lesion counting in her office notes, starting in the 1930s.[135] Several systems for grading the severity of acne currently exist.

In 1956, Pillsbury, Shelley and Kligman published the earliest known grading system [133] The grading includes the following

- Grade 1: Comedones and occasional small cysts confined to the face.
- Grade 2: Comedones with occasional pustules and small cysts confined to the face.
- Grade 3: Many comedones and small and large inflammatory papules and pustules, more extensive but confined to the face.
- Grade 4: Many comedones and deep lesions tend to coalesce and canalize, and involve the face and the upper aspects of the trunk
- In 1958, James and Tisserand in their review of acne therapy, provided an alternative grading scheme[133]
- Grade 1: Simple non-inflammatory acne - comedones and a few papules.
- Grade 2: Comedones, papules and a few pustules.
- Grade 3: Larger inflammatory papules, pustules and a few cysts; a more severe form involving the face, neck and upper portions of the trunk.
- Grade 4: More severe, with cysts becoming confluent.
- Acne vulgaris was graded by Indian authors,[134] using a simple grading system, which classifies acne vulgaris into four grades as follows.
- Grade 1: Comedones, occasional papules.
- Grade 2: Papules, comedones, few pustules.
- Grade 3: Predominant pustules, nodules, abscesses.
- Grade 4: Mainly cysts, abscesses, widespread scarring.

3. Current treatment of acne

Despite the negative impacts of acne vulgaris, treatment compliance is poor because of numerous factors.[135] Adolescents discontinue treatment, in part, because of early improvement, perception of worsening acne, and side effects, especially with topical treatments, suggesting that anticipatory guidance and mitigation of side effects may improve compliance. Treatment with oral isotretinoin and satisfaction with treatment have been linked with increased acne treatment compliance in adolescents[136] which suggests that treatment simplification (often monotherapy), patient selection, and increased acne severity associated with isotretinoin use may contribute to increased compliance.

Conversely, prescription of multiple treatments, topical retinoids, and recommendation of treatment with over-the-counter products have been associated with primary noncompliance in adolescents with acne,[137] a challenge given that current acne guidelines include topical retinoids as a mainstay of treatment and recommend against monotherapy with the currently available medications.[138]In addition, cost has been identified as a barrier to treatment in adult patients[139] although its effect on parents of adolescents is less clear. Authors of only one study assessed an interventional method aimed at improving adolescent compliance with acne treatment. A randomized control study (N = 40 patients) of an automated text message reminder system did not yield increased compliance with topical acne treatment in adolescents (33.9% in reminder group versus 36.5% in control group) after 12 weeks.[140]

i. Topical Retinoids

Topical retinoids are a diverse group of vitamin A derivatives that modulate gene expression. The US Food and Drug Administration (FDA)–approved topical retinoids for the treatment of acne vulgaris, including adapalene , tretinoin, and tazarotene, prevent comedone formation by regulating keratinocyte proliferation and differentiation; they also have antiinflammatory effects.[141] Topical retinoids are the preferred treatment and maintenance therapy for all acne, decreasing both comedonal and inflammatory acne lesion counts.[142] They also help prevent and reduce the appearance of atrophic scars[143] and dyspigmentation.[144]

Because of common and limiting side effects of dryness, irritation, redness, and peeling, retinoid-naive patients are typically started on low concentrations of topical adapalene or tretinoin and escalated stepwise to higher concentrations or to tazarotene as needed and tolerated. However, there remains a paucity of comprehensive comparative non–industry- sponsored randomized controlled head-to-head studies of the various topical retinol formulations[145] Therefore, the clinical teaching that tazarotene is the most effective and most poorly tolerated retinoid whereas adapalene is the least effective and best-tolerated retinoid is not well grounded in generalizable evidence and is an area for further study..

Examples-retinol, tretinoin, adapalene, tazarotene, alitretinoin, and bexarotene.

Topical and Oral Antibiotics and Benzoyl Peroxide

Topical antibiotics can be used in the first-line treatment of acne vulgaris and have additional antiinflammatory effects[144] but should not be used as monotherapy because of the rapid development of high rates of antibiotic resistance after weeks to months [144,145,148] High rates of resistance of Cute Bacterium acnes, formerly known as Propionibacterium acnes, to erythromycin and clindamycin have been reported globally.[146,147,149] Increased resistance correlates with decreased efficacy for acne treatment.[150]

Resistance may persist after treatment is discontinued, and resistant C acnes strains have been found in untreated contacts.[147]Furthermore, high rates of resistance of colonizer Staphylococcus aureus to erythromycin and clindamycin (44% and 40%, respectively) in patients with acne have been reported.[151] This is of special concern given the potential for serious infections caused by multidrug-resistant S aureus strains. Studies reveal reduced rates of resistance of C acnes and Staphylococcus epidermidis with concomitant benzoyl peroxide use,[152,148] likely because of its nonselective bactericidal activity.Hence, current guidelines recommend use of topical antibiotics in combination with benzoyl peroxide either as a rinse-off or leave-on product.[144,145] Oral antibiotics are indicated for the treatment of moderate to severe inflammatory acne or inflammatory acne recalcitrant to topical therapy alone[144,145]They should be used in combination with topical retinoids and/or benzoyl peroxide; monotherapy is not recommended.[144,145]Therapy should be temporary, as a bridge to other oral therapies or to topical medications alone[144,145]Long-term treatment (.3–6 months) should be avoided to limit the development of antibiotic resistance [144,145,146]The tetracyclines, namely doxycycline and minocycline, have antiinflammatory properties and are considered first-line oral antibiotic therapy per US guidelines[145] Rates of S aureus resistance to tetracyclines (,10%) in patients with acne who are treated with antibiotics are far lower than those to clindamycin and erythromycin.[151]Sarecycline, a novel tetracycline with narrow-spectrum activity, was FDA approved in October 2018 for the treatment of moderate to severe inflammatory acne in patients 9 years of age and older [153] Oral macrolides, such as azithromycin, may be used for patients in whom tetracyclines are contraindicated, although use of erythromycin should be restricted because of high rates of resistance. Treatment with other classes of antibiotics used in acne, including trimethoprim and sulfamethoxazole, trimethoprim, penicillin, and cephalosporins, is discouraged because of limited supporting evidence, unless tetracyclines and macrolides are contraindicated.[145] If repeat treatment with oral antibiotics is needed, some recommend avoiding class switching unless otherwise justified to reduce the risk of antibacterial resistance.[146],[154] It is reasonable to try an alternate class of antibiotics if a patient fails first-line therapy.

iii. Hormonal therapies

Currently, there are two main types of hormonal therapies (HT): first, the group of noncontraceptive hormonal therapies, which include the following drugs: spironolactone, cyproterone acetate, and flutamide; and second, the hormonal contraceptives, which include different drugs that have a similar chemical structure composed by two molecules: an estrogen and a progestogen. Based on evidence, the Food and Drug Administration from the United States (US FDA) has approved the following associations of estrogen and progestin drugs for management of acne[155]

- Ethinyl-estradiol 20/30/35 µg and norethindrone 1 mg.
- Ethinyl-estradiol 35 µg and norgestimate 180/ 215/250 µg.
- Ethinyl-estradiol 20 µg and drospirenone 3 mg. Besides the above associations, in other countries such as Canada, more combinations are approved for acne management:
- Ethinyl-estradiol 35 µg and cyproterone acetate 2 mg.
- Ethinyl-estradiol 35 µg and levonorgestrel 100 µg
- Ethinyl-estradiol 35 µg and drospirenone 3 mg. The most relevant features of each HT are presented below.

. Summarization of current available hormonal therapies
Pharmacology
COCsa
Spironolactone
Cyproterone acetate
Flutamide
Mechanism of action

- 5-Alpha reductase activity
- Free testosterone
- Sebaceous gland activity
- Size of the gland

- 5-Alpha reductase activity
- Free testosterone
- Testosterone and dihydrotestostero ne binding
- Sebaceous gland activity

- Blocks receptor of testosterone
- Secretion of gonadotropins

- Blocks receptor of testosterone
- Secretion of gonadotropins

Side effects

- GI disorders

- Hyperkalemia

- GI disorders

- GI disorders

profile

- Spotting
- Headache
- Breast tenderness
- Fluid retention
- Depression

Hypercalcemia

- Breast tenderness
- Menstrual irregularities
- Hypotension
- Reduced libid

- Headache
- Breast tenderness
- Menstrual irregularities
- Fluid retention
- Liver dysfunction
- Blood clotting disorders

- Hematological disorders
- Muscle cramps
- Gynecomastia
- Acute liver failure

Contraindication s

- Smoking in

age >35
• Cardiovascular disease
• Hematological disorders

- BMI ≥35

  ◦ Migraine
  ◦ Risk of estrogen dependent malignancy

Risk of estrogen dependentMonit oring tests malignancy

- History of meningioma • Liver disease • Malignancy (other than prostatic cancer)
- Hematological disorders

- Severe diabetes
- Sickle cell anemia
- Chronic severe depression

Liver disease
Monitoring tests
No needed unless patients have risk factors
Kalemia

- Blood pressure
- ECG (when high dose is used)

- Liver function
- Clotting factors

Liver function

4. Diet in treated and untreated acne

- Milk and dairy products

The first studies on this issue have been conducted in the 40s of the last century, however until today there has been no conclusive evidence that milk and dairy products have comedogenic effects. The probable cause of possible comedogenic effects of milk and its products is the content of hormones produced by cows during pregnancy. It is believed that the constituent of milk that mostly stimulates the pilosebaceous unit is insulin-like growth factor 1 (IGF-1), whose concentration in the blood varies depending on the severity of acne[156]. High plasma levels of IGF-1 which are caused by consumption of milk, stimulates proliferation of sebocytes, resulting in the development and progression of acne lesions [158]. Decrease in fasting insulin and postprandial insulin and IGF-1 reduces the production of sebum and keratinocyte proliferation thereby reducing the number of acne lesions. Insulin- like growth factor 1 increases sensitivity of the adrenal gland to adrenocorticotropic hormone and induces the expression and activity of key enzymes involved in the biosynthesis of adrenal androgens [157]. Insulin-like growth factor 1 also stimulates the synthesis of androgens by ovaries and testicles and inhibits hepatic synthesis of sex hormone binding globulin (SHBG), which in effect increases bioavailability of androgens. Both IGF-1 and androgens stimulate sebum production, which is one of the pathogenic factors of acne formation [159].

- Chocolate

Chocolate has always been considered as a factor that may contribute to exacerbation of acne, but there is a very limited amount of evidence supporting its negative impact on the skin. Dermatologists often observe that patients have new pimples a few days after ingestion of products containing chocolate [160].However there is no information about the type of chocolate consumed by subjects and the percentage of cocoa in consumed samples, which can influence results. Dark chocolate contains more antioxidants than milk chocolate, which would lead to the conclusion that it may have much smaller comedogenic effects. However this issue still remains unclear. As to the question of whether chocolate aggravates acne lesions, there is still no clear answer. [160,161]

- Glycemic index

It is believed that glycemic load and glycemic index of the whole diet may participate in pathogenesis of acne vulgaris. The most vulnerable is consumption of products based on their high values. Diet based on products with a high glycemic index leads to hyperinsulinemia.Elevated insulin levels stimulate the secretion of androgens and cause an increased production of sebum, which plays a fundamental role in pathogenesis of acne vulgaris [160,162] Hyperinsulinemia affects the level of circulating IGF-1 and insulin-growth factor binding protein (IGFBP-3), which directly affect keratinocyte proliferation and apoptosis. In hyperinsulinemia, the level of IGF-1 increases whereas the level of IGFBP-3 decreases, which leads to an imbalance. As a result, keratinocyte proliferation increases. Insulin-like growth factor 1 influences comedogenic factors such as androgens, growth hormone and glucocorticoids.

- Dietary fiber

There are no clinical studies that clearly illustrate the effect of dietary fiber intake on the course of acne vulgaris. In a Kaufman study, in which patients with acne vulgaris consumed 30 g of high fiber breakfast cereal (13 g fiber/ serving), a significant improvement in the skin condition was shown [163]. In Smith *et al.* study, after introduction of a low glycemic load diet, improvement in the skin condition was noticed. Researchers suggested that it could be an effect of large amounts of dietary fiber in this kind of diet. [164]

- Fatty acids

The ratio of omega-6 to omega-3 fatty acids resulting from diet is one of the factors that modulate the inflammatory mechanism. A high intake of omega-3 fatty acids can inhibit the production of proinflammatory cytokines which can have a therapeutic effect on acne vulgaris [165]

- Antioxidants

Reactive oxygen species produced by neutrophils participate in inflammatory progression of acne. Reactive oxygen species are normally removed by cellular antioxidants such as glucose-6-phosphate dehydrogenase and catalase, both of which are presented in small quantities in patients with acne. It has been suggested that oxidative stress may be implicated in the origin of acne and that drugs with antioxidant effects (or antioxidant supplements) may be valuable adjuvants in acne treatment.[165]

Studies mentioned above are crucial to support the theory of the positive role of antioxidants in acne therapy, but effects of these substances in the course of this disease are not yet fully explored.

Zinc

Zinc is a micronutrient that is essential for the development and functioning of the human skin. It has been shown to be bacteriostatic against *Propionibacterium acnes*, to inhibit chemotaxis and to reduce production of pro-inflammatory cytokine – tumor necrosis factor α (TNF-α) .[166]

- Vitamin A

Vitamin A is a group of compounds which can be found in both animal and plant products. Retinol and its derivatives are found mainly in products of animal origin, while products of plant origin contain mainly provitamin A . Its main sources are milk and dairy products, eggs, liver, fish and oils derived from them. Vitamin A is fat-soluble vitamin stored in the liver. [167]

- Iodine

iodine is a nutrient that is essential for the proper organism functioning. Acne that occurs after ingestion of foods rich in iodine appears suddenly and is characterized by many papules. It has been hypothesized that the association between acne and milk may be a result of the iodine content of milk which can vary with time of year, location, supplementation of animal feed and use of iodophor-sanitizing solutions [166]

Lasers/Light-Based Technology for the Treatment of Acne

Over almost a century, many types of light sources were introduced in the hope to treat/improve acne symptoms. These light sources include fluorescent, halogen, xenon, tungsten lamps, and recently lasers. Light-induced inactivation of dye-labeled bacteria by photodynamic reactions was pioneered by vonTappeiner and Jodlbaurin in 1904.[167] In 1924, Passow and Rimpau[168] found a higher photodynamic inactivation rate in Gram-positive bacteria versus Gram Negative bacteria.

The first light sources for the treatment of acne were conventional lamps where the output was defined by the use of filters. A drawback with this was that calculating the delivered light dose was difficult. High-intensity visible light phototherapy for acne was described by Meffert et al[169] but they used a light source emitting not only visible light but also ultraviolet A (UVA) comprising up to 15% to 20% of the total irradiation dose. Sigurdsson et al.[170] usedPhilips HPM–10,400 W combined with an NUVILEX 390-nm filter (Desag, Germany) that filters most but not all UVA harmful rays.The spectrum of their lamp peaked at 420 nm and had two other small peaks of emission at 405 and 435 nm. Their apparatus emitted at 40 cm, 0.5 J/cm2 of UVA, 20 J/cm2 of violet/ blue, and 5 J/cm2 of green light. Recently, a newly developed high-intensity, enhanced, narrow-band, blue-light source (CureLight) was introduced for the treatment of mild to moderate acne. This apparatus uses high-intensity, 400-W, enhanced blue light, a metal halide lamp, plus double UV-cut filters with the emitting peak of 407 to 420 nm, which produces 90 mW/cm2 homogeneous illumination over an area of 20-20 cm2 .The system destroys the P. acnes bacteria in facial, back, and chest sebaceous glands by targeting the porphyrins in the bacteria. Last summer, the system was cleared by the Food and Drug Administration to market for acne treatment. Another light-based acne clearance system is ClearTouch. The system is a broad-spectrum (430 to 1200 nm) flash lamp light source.The system uses the yellow and green bands (500 to 600 nm) to allow greater skin penetration (several mm) but has a lower extinction coefficient Q Band. Food and Drug Administration approval is pending.While the previous two light-based systems target P. acnes, a secondary effect of acne, Smoothbeam diode laser targets the sebaceous glands.The Smoothbeam uses a 1450-nm wavelength to alter the sebaceous glands thermally at the sites of the acne lesions. Laser energy from the device is absorbed by the water in the upper papillary dermis where the sebaceous gland resides.The heat from the absorbed energy creates a thermal injury and alters the structure of the sebaceous glands.Non Pustular acne can be treated with the PhotoGenica V pulsed-dye laser. The device emits light of 595-nm wavelength that is absorbed by the oxyhemoglobin. The technology claims to improve the erythema that acne causes.Currently, PDT is being used with 5- aminolevulinic acid, in conjunction with different light wavelengths.When delivered to target tissues, 5-aminolevulinic acid is taken up and converted into protoporphyrin IX, a potent photosensitizer, which can be then activated by an appropriate light source.[171] Light Source Manufacturer Model Parameters Target/Chromophore

- Fluorescent lamps
- Light Source
- Green light
- Violet light
- Blue metal halide lamp
- Xenon flash lamp
- Lasers

CHAPTER II

LITERATURE HISTORY

1. **Anna Hwee Sing Heng *et al,*(2020);** A systematic review was conducted on epidemiology studies on acne obtained from a Web of Science search to study risk factors associated with acne presentation and severity. A strong association was observed between several risk factors – family history, age, BMI and skin type – and acne presentation or severity in multiple studies. The pooled odds ratio of 2.36 (95% CI 1.97–2.83) for overweight/ obese BMI with reference to normal/underweight BMI and the pooled odds ratio of 2.91 (95% CI 2.58–3.28) for family history in parents with reference to no family history in parents demonstrate this strong association. In addition, a pooled odds ratio of 1.07 (95% CI 0.42– 2.71) was obtained for sex (males with reference to females). However, the association between other factors, such as dietary factors and smoking, and acne presentation or severity was less clear, with inconsistent results between studies. Thus, further research is required to understand how these factors may influence the development and severity of acne. This study summarizes the potential factors that may affect the risk of acne presentation or severe acne and can help researchers and clinicians to understand the epidemiology of acne and severe acne. Furthermore, the findings can direct future acne research, with the hope of gaining insight into the pathophysiology of acne so as to develop effective acne treatments.[172]

2. **Kaiane A. Habeshian,*et al* (2020);** Acne vulgaris is an extraordinarily common skin condition in adolescents. The mainstays of acne treatment have remained largely unchanged over recent years. In the context of increasing antibiotic resistance worldwide, there is a global movement away from antibiotic monotherapy toward their more restrictive use. Classically reserved for nodulocystic acne, isotretinoin has become the drug of choice by dermatologists for moderate to severe acne. Given the virtually ubiquitous nature of acne in teenagers, there remains an appreciable need for novel therapies. In this article, we will cover the currently used acne treatments, evaluate the issues and data supporting their use, explore the issues of compliance and the mental health implications of acne care, and recommend directions for the field of acne management in adolescents in the years ahead.[173]

3. **Tian-Xin Cong [1]*et al* (2019);** Acne vulgaris is a cutaneous chronic inflammatory disorder with complex pathogenesis. Four factors play vital roles in acne pathophysiology: hyperseborrhea and dysmenorrhea, altered keratinization of the pilosebaceous duct, Cutibacterium acnes (C. acnes) and inflammation. The main hormones responsible for the development of acne vulgaris include androgens, insulin and insulin-like growth factor-1Other factors involved in this process are corticotropin-releasing hormone, α-melanocyte- stimulating hormone and substance P. Wnt/β-catenin signaling pathway, phosphoinositide 3- kinase (PI3K)/ Akt pathway, mitogen-activated protein kinase pathway, adenosine 5′- monophosphate-activated protein kinase pathway and nuclear factor kappa B pathway participate in the modulation of sebocyte, keratinocyte and inflammatory cell (e.g. lymphocytes, monocytes, macrophages, neutrophils) activity. Among all the triggers and pathways mentioned above, IGF-1-induced PI3K/Akt/Forkhead box protein O1/mammalian target of rapamycin (mTOR) C1 pathway is the most important signaling responsible for acne pathogenesis. Commonly used anti-acne agents include retinoids, benzoyl peroxide, antibiotics and hormonal agents (e.g. spironolactone, combination oral contraceptive and flutamide). New approaches including peroxisome proliferator-activated receptor γ modifier, melanocortin receptor antagonists, epigallocatechin-3-gallate, metformin, olumacostat glasaretil, stearoyl-CoA desaturase inhibitor omiganan pentahydrochloride, KDPT, afamelanotide, apremilast and biologics have been developed as promising treatments for acne vulgaris. Although these anti-acne agents have various pharmacological effects against the diverse pathogenesis of acne, all of them have a synergistic mode of action, the attenuation of Akt/ mTORC1 signaling and enhancement of p53 signal transduction. In addition to drug therapy, a diet with no hyperglycemic carbohydrates, no milk and dairy products is also beneficial for treatment of acne.[174]

4. **Husein Husein-ElAhmed,(2015);** Acne vulgaris is a very common condition affecting up to 93% of adolescents. Although rare, this disease may persist in adulthood. In adult women with acne (those older than 25 years old), this condition is particularly relevant because of the refractory to conventional therapies, which makes acne a challenge for dermatologists in this group of patients. In order to reduce its potential risk for chronicity and the involvement of visible anatomical sites such as face and upper torso, acne has been associated with a wide spectrum of psychological and social dysfunction such as depression, anxiety, suicidal ideation, somatization, and social inhibition. In particular, adult women with acne have been shown to be adversely impacted by the effect of acne on their quality of life. For the last four decades, dermatologists have used hormonal therapies for the management of acne vulgaris in adult women, which are considered a rational choice given the severity and chronicity of this condition in this group of patients. The aim of this work is to review the hormonal drugs for management of acne. [175]

5. **Sara Moradi Tuchayi** *et al*,**(2015)** ; Acne vulgaris is a chronic inflammatory disease — rather than a natural part of the life cycle as colloquially viewed — of the pilosebaceous unit (comprising the hair follicle, hair shaft and sebaceous gland) and is among the most common dermatological conditions worldwide. Some of the key mechanisms involved in the development of acne include disturbed sebaceous gland activity associated with hyperseborrhea (that is, increased sebum production) and alterations in sebum fatty acid composition, dysregulation of the hormone microenvironment, interaction with neuropeptides, follicular hyperkeratinization, induction of inflammation and dysfunction of the innate and adaptive immunity. Grading of acne involves lesion counting and photographic methods. However, there is a lack of consensus on the exact grading criteria, which hampers the conduction and comparison of randomized controlled clinical trials evaluating treatments. Prevention of acne relies on the successful management of modifiable risk factors, such as underlying systemic diseases and lifestyle factors. Several treatments are available, but guidelines suffer from a lack of data to make evidence-based recommendations. In addition, the complex combination treatment regimens required to target different aspects of acne pathophysiology lead to poor adherence, which undermines treatment success. Acne commonly causes scarring and reduces the quality of life of patients. New treatment options with a shift towards targeting the early processes involved in acne development instead of suppressing the effects of end products will enhance our ability to improve the outcomes for patients with acne.[176]

6. **Bodo C Melnik(2015);**acne vulgaris, an epidemic inflammatory skin disease of adolescence, is closely related to Western diet. Three major food classes that promote acne are: 1) hyperglycemic carbohydrates, 2) milk and dairy products, 3) saturated fats including *trans*-fats and deficient ω-3 polyunsaturated fatty acids (PUFAs). Diet-induced insulin/insulin-like growth factor (IGF-1)-signaling is superimposed on elevated IGF-1 levels during puberty, thereby unmasking the impact of aberrant nutrigenomics on sebaceous gland homeostasis. Western diet provides abundant branched-chain amino acids (BCAAs), glutamine, and palmitic acid. Insulin and IGF-1 suppress the activity of the metabolic transcription factor forkhead box O1 (FoxO1). Insulin, IGF-1, BCAAs, glutamine, and palmitate activate the nutrient-sensitive kinase mechanistic target of rapamycin complex 1 (mTORC1), the key regulator of anabolism and lipogenesis. FoxO1 is a negative coregulatorof androgen receptor, peroxisome proliferator-activated receptor-γ (PPARγ), liver X receptor- α, and sterol response element binding protein-1c (SREBP-1c), crucial transcription factors of sebaceous lipogenesis. mTORC1 stimulates the expression of PPARγ and SREBP-1c, promoting sebum production. SREBP-1c upregulates stearoyl-CoA- and Δ6-desaturase, enhancing the proportion of monounsaturated fatty acids in sebum triglycerides. Diet- mediated aberrations in sebum quantity (hyperseborrhea) and composition (dysmenorrhea) promote *Propionibacterium acnes* overgrowth and biofilm formation with overexpression of the virulence factor triglyceride lipase increasing follicular levels of free palmitate and oleate. Free palmitate functions as a "danger signal," stimulating toll-like receptor-2-mediated inflammasome activation with interleukin-1β release, Th17 differentiation, and interleukin-17-mediated keratinocyte proliferation. Oleate stimulates *P. acnes* adhesion, keratinocyte proliferation, and comedogenesis via interleukin-1α release. Thus, diet-induced metabolic alterations promote the visible sebo follicular inflammasome pathway acne vulgaris. Nutrition therapy of acne has to increase FoxO1 and to attenuate mTORC1/SREBP-1c signaling. Patients should balance total calorie uptake and restrict refined carbohydrates,

milk, dairy protein supplements, saturated fats, and *trans*-fats. A paleolithic-like diet enriched in vegetables and fish is recommended. Plant-derived mTORC1 inhibitors and ω-3-PUFAs are promising dietary supplements supporting nutrition therapy of acne vulgaris.[177]

7. **Manoj A. Suva1** *et al***(2014);** Acne vulgaris is one of the most common dermatological disorders that afflict people in their adolescence. Acne vulgaris or simply known as acne is a human skin disease characterized by skin with scaly red skin (seborrhea), blackheads and whiteheads (comedones), pinheads (papules), large papules (nodules), pimples and scarring. Acne vulgaris is a disease of the pilosebaceous unit characterized by the formation of open and closed comedones, papules, pustules, nodules and cysts. Acne affects skin having dense sebaceous follicles in areas including face, chest and back. Acne is not life threatening but severe acne can affect psychological status and social activities. The present review focuses on epidemiology, etiology, pathogenesis, diagnosis, differential diagnosis and management of acne with the pharmaceutical dosage forms of oral and topical administrations. Various medicines for acne treatment includes benzoyl peroxide, antibiotics, antiseborrheic medications, sulfur and sodium Sulfacetamide, antiandrogen medications, salicylic acid, hormonal treatments, alpha hydroxy acid, retinoids, azelaic acid, keratolytic soaps andnicotinamide. Currently laser and light devices and minor subcision surgery have been also performed for acne treatment.[178]

8. **Hanieh Azimi** *et al***,(2012) ;** Aim: This review focuses on plants currently used and those with a high potency for the future development of anti-acne products. Methods: All relevant literature databases were searched up to 25 March 2011. The search terms were plant, herb, herbal therapy, phytotherapy, and acne, acne vulgaris and anti-acne. All of the human, animal, and in vitro studies, and reviews were included. Anti-bacterial, antiinflammatory, anti-oxidant, and anti-androgen effects were the key outcomes. Results: Studies on cell lines revealed that flavonoid, alkaloid, essential oil, phenol and phenolic compound, tannin, xanthone and xanthone derivative, and the bisnaphthquione derivative are effective in treatment of acne. Animal studies showed that diterpene acid, phenylpropanoid glycosides, acteoside and flavonoids have anti-inflammatory activity. Eleven human studies revealed that Camellia sinensis has 5α-reductase inhibitory and antiinflammatory activities. Also anti- bacterial effect was shown by oleoresin of Commiphora mukul. Conclusion: In addition to the standardization of these herbs, screening herbs as anti-acne agents may help to find new sources of therapy for acne.[179]

9. **Hywel C Williams** *et al***,(2011) ;** Acne is a chronic inflammatory disease of the pilosebaceous unit resulting from androgen-induced increased sebum production, altered keratinisation, inflammation, and bacterial colonisation of hair follicles on the face, neck, chest, and back by Propionibacterium acnes. Although early colonisation with P acnes and family history might have important roles in the disease, exactly what triggers acne and how treatment affects the course of the disease remain unclear. Other factors such as diet have been implicated, but not proven. Facial scarring due to acne affects up to 20% of teenagers. Acne can persist into adulthood, with detrimental effects on self-esteem. There is no ideal treatment for acne, although a suitable regimen for reducing lesions can be found for most patients. Good quality evidence on comparative effectiveness of common topical and systemic acne therapies is scarce. Topical therapies including benzoyl peroxide, retinoids, and antibiotics when used in combination usually improve control of mild to moderate acne. Treatment with combined oral contraceptives can help women with acne. Patients with more severe inflammatory acne usually need oral antibiotics combined with topical benzoyl peroxide to decrease antibiotic-resistant organisms. Oral isotretinoin is the most effective therapy and is used early in severe disease, although its use is limited by teratogenicity and other side-effects. Availability, adverse effects, and cost, limit the use of photodynamic therapy. New research is needed into the therapeutic comparative effectiveness and safety of the many products available, and to better understand the natural history, subtypes, and triggers of acne.[180]

10. **Sanjay K Rathi(2011);** Acne Vulgaris is one of the most common skin disorders which dermatologists have to treat. It mainly affects adolescents, though it may present at any age. In recent years, due to better understanding of the pathogenesis of acne, new therapeutic modalities and various permutations and combinations have been designed. Topical agents; benzoyl peroxide, antibiotics, retinoids, etc are the mainstay of treatment; can be given in combinations. While systemic therapy includes oral antibiotics, hormonal therapy, and isotretinoin, depending upon the need of patients it has to be selected. Physical treatment in the form of lesion removal, photo-therapy

is also helpful in few of them. Since various old and new topical and systemic agents are available to treat acne, it sometimes confuses dermatologists. To overcome this, a panel of physicians and researchers worked together as a global alliance and task force to improve outcomes in acne treatment. They have tried to give consensus recommendations for the treatment of acne. Successful management of acne needs careful selection of anti-acne agents according to clinical presentation and individual patient needs.[181]

CHAPTER III

Research Methodology

Acne vulgaris or simply known as acne is a human skin disease characterized by skin with scaly red skin (seborrhea), blackheads and whiteheads (comedones), pinheads (papules), large papules (nodules), pimples and scarring . Acne affects skin having dense sebaceous follicles in areas including face, chest and back. Acne may be of inflammatory or non- inflammatory forms. Due to changes in pilosebaceous units lesions are caused by androgen stimulation. Acne occurs commonly during adolescence, affecting about 80–90% of teenagers in the Western world and lower rates are reported in rural societies . Acne is usually caused by an increase in androgens levels like testosterone mainly during puberty in both male and females . Acne reduces over time and tends to disappear over the age . The large nodules are called cysts and severe inflammatory acne is called nodulocystic.

The effect of acne on the emotional state of the patient

The emotional impact of acne can be difficult to predict. The impact on a given patient can be influenced by many factors including age, psychosocial developmental period, baseline self- esteem and coping abilities, clinical severity of the disease, family and peer support systems, personality coping styles and/or disorders, and other underlying psychopathology.

1. Emotional impact of acne

    - Anxiety
    - Depression
    - Frustration
    - Anger
    - Impairment in self-image

2. Psychosocial problems associated with acne

    - Decreased dating, sports, and eating
    - out Impaired academic performance
    - Increased unemployment rates

3. Frequently encountered characteristics of the high-risk patient

    - Impaired interpersonal skills
    - Disrupted family functioning
    - Recent change in peer group
    - academic/vocational functioning

4. Specific behavioral and emotional characteristics of the high-risk patient.

    - Poor eye contact
    - Limited verbal productivity
    - Suicidal or homicidal ideation or intent Self-mutilating behaviors Hallucinations or delusional

- Compulsive or ritualistic behaviors including excessive picking Intense feelings of depression, agitation, anger, irritability
- High levels of anxiety or agitation
- Poor self-care and personal hygiene
- Angry or negative verbalizations

2 Current treatment failures on acne vulgaris.

- Antibiotic resistance in acne-

The systemic use of antimicrobials in acne has been the mainstay of therapy since its first introduction by George Clinton Andrews, Jr. (1891-1978) and his team in 1951. In the following decade, Marion B. Sulzberger (1895-1983) and his group had developed the present-day use of tetracycline. With the advent of chlortetracycline (Aureomycin®), tetracycline became an important part of the acne regimen .Oxytetracycline (Terramycin®) was generated from Streptomyces rimosus mainly for topical use. Other tetracycline's were identified later, including semisynthetic derivatives such as doxycycline and minocycline and some natural products such as tetracyclines from S. aureofaciens, S. rimosus, and S. aureofaciens. Antimicrobials are thought not only to reduce the bacterial load but also to work substantially in an antiinflammatory manner .

- Topical retinoids and their side effects-

Many topical retinoids like *retinol, tretinoin, adapalene, tazarotene, alitretinoin, and bexarotene.* Having a good effect on acne but they contains such side effects like

- Redness.
- Drying and/or peeling of skin.
- Skin hot to touch.
- Swelling.
- Blistering (a raised portion of skin that is filled with fluid)
- Pruritus (itching)
- Worsening of acne that usually resolves.
- Increased sensitivity to heat and cold.
- Erythema (a type of skin rash caused by injured or inflamed blood capillaries.)
- Xerosis
- stinging
- Pregnancy category X.

Due to which they may not be an appropriate option for the treatment of acne vulgaris.

- Scars produced by laser therapy.

i. Superficial macular scars- Commitment of the epidermis and superficial dermis clinically shows macular pigment and erythema.
ii. Ice-pick scars- This type of scar has cone shaped. The surface is generally wider than its infundibulum, which is aimed at deeper layers of skin .It goes deeper until the reticular dermis and sometimes until the subcutaneous tissue. These scars are difficult to treat because they are very deep, this is the reason why these

types of scars do not respond to many treatments.

iii. Rolling scars- The shape of this type of scars is corrugated (wavy): There is a junction fibrous dermo-hypodermic defective, due to damaged subcutaneous fat.

iv. Boxcar scars- These have an oval shape. The diameter of the surface is greater than its depth. It varies in depth within 0.1–0.5 mm and more variable length up to 4 mm diameter.

i. Hypertrophic scars- Characterized by Increase tissue in the scar periphery, these scars can also have a spontaneous remission Keloids Disproportionate excess tissue outside the boundaries of the initial injury. They are not commonly caused by acne.

- Hormonal therapy not a first line treatment

Several misconceptions regarding the use of OCs need to be addressed:

Combined OCs do not cause weight gain.- Teenagers often do not comply with the use of OCs because they believe that they cause weight gain; however, weight gain was similar in patients receiving OC compared with placebo.

Risk of cancer. Treatment with OCs has been associated with a small increased risk of cervical cancer, although some studies link this risk to women positive for human papillomavirus infection.

- Benzoyl peroxide-

Benzoyl peroxide works by peeling away the skin to get rid of dead skin cells, excessive oil, and bacteria that may be trapped underneath. Such effects can lead to dryness, as well as redness and excessive peeling. You might notice itching and general irritation at the site of application too.Due to the current treatment failures or long term side effects and resistance of antibiotics The treatment of acne vulgaris is not successful.The risk of ovarian cancer inm hormonal therapy side effects of retinoids and remaining scars of laser treatment.So due to these conditions one of the best options is herbal therapy which is done by various herbal drugs gone through clinical trials. And shown effectiveness in acne vulgaris. And the best part of herbal drugs is that it is obtained naturally and has no side effects or very few which has no direct impact on daily life.In this clinical review other than presenting the possible causes of acne vulgaris and its available drugs, recently published papers about medicinal plants used in the treatment of acne vulgaris are reviewed. In this study, I attempted to present information from studiespublished since early 1980, which were present in databases such as Google scholar, PubMed related to medicinal plants effective in the treatment of acne vulgaris.Benefits of herbals on acne -Herbal medicines are gaining increased popularity due to their advantages, such as better patient tolerance, long history of use, fewer side-effects and being relatively less expensive. Many medicinal plants with anti-inflammation and antibacterial activities are used in different ways in the treatment of acne and other infectious diseases.Some are antibacterial in nature, some are anti-inflammatory properties that some herbs have to boost your skin's capacity to manage external damage and thus avoid sensitivity issues. When sourced organically, these natural remedies can really make a difference to your anti- acne skincare routine.Studies were included in the present systematic review if they met these criteria: to begin with full-text publication was written in English, in addition inspected the Anti acne effect of plants on acne vulgaris and, finally reported the percentage of efficiency or complete prevention time. Following studies were excluded: studies exploring the repellency effect of chemical-based products, studies examining the anti acne effect of plants on going clinical trails. articles without full texts, reviews, duplicate articles, abstracts, republished data, comments, conference papers, editorials, and studies with insufficient data.

After identifying the eligible studies, the following data were collected from each study by application of standardized data collection form to improve accuracy and critical appraisal: the first author name, country of origin, journal details, publication year, condition of study (field or laboratory), plant name, and duration of time taken to treat acne. All data were independently extracted by two reviewers and disagreements were solved by discussion, and if necessary, a third author was involved.

A total of 242 studies were found by the initial literature search of the databases. Of the 242 excluded citations, 80 were duplicated studies; 94 were not relevant to the anti acne effect. After screening titles/abstracts; 26 were review publications; 8 investigated the antiacne impact of chemical-based antibiotics, anti inflammatory, topical retinoids and hormonal contraceptives 7 studies were conducted on laboratory animals; 12 were abstracts, conference papers, comments, and editorials; 10 studies had not reported sufficient data regarding the percentage of anti acne effect and, 5 studies were other irrelevant studies. The included studies were published between 1999 and 2021.

CHAPTER IV

Result and Discussion

Result-Clinical trials of plant having anti acne activity

In this review, i collected and described plants that can be efficient in treatment of acne vulgaris. These plants can have anti-acne effects because of four mechanisms including anti- bacterial, anti-inflammatory, anti-oxidant and antiandrogen activities. A most of the plants were gone through randomized clinical trails The plants with essential oils are mainly extracted by hexane Phenolic compounds reveal a dose dependent anti-oxidant activity that is directly related to the amount of total phenolic contents . In addition, a polyphenol-rich extract could have anti-androgen effect. In addition, a polyphenol-rich extract could have anti-androgen effect. And some plants contaning 5alpha reductase activity . The fancy of beauty is natural, and cosmetics are as ancient as mankind and civilization . Therefore, acne vulgaris could suppress an individual's self-confidence with regard to physical appearances or even depression that may affect all aspects of life. In view of increasing resistance to existing anti-microbial agents, side effects and sometimes high cost of treatment , discovering an effective treatment for acne that is well tolerated by the patients is a challenge. The use of natural remedies dates back thousands of years. It is estimated that there are 250,000–500,000species of plants on Earth which offers a great hope in the identification of phytotherapeutic agents and their development into drugs for the treatment of acne vulgaris that affects approximately 80% of the population between the ages of 12–25 years. In addition, recent studies have indicated herbal medicines that are strong antioxidants have many positive effects in oxidant related diseases.

S.no	Plant part and family	Plant part	Extraction n solvent	Active compound	Clinical study design	No of patient	Duration of treatment	Effect	Ref
01	*Aloe barbadensis* (*Asphodelaceae*)	Leaf	Pure aloe vera gel	Aloesin	A randomized ed double bind placebo-controlled group design	53	4 w	Anti-bacterial and anti-inflammatory	182
02	*Azadirachta indica* (*meliaceae*)	Leaves and bark	Petroleum ether	polyphenol	A randomized ed double bind placebo-controlled group design	53	4 w	Anti-bacterial and anti-inflammatory	182
03	*Curcuma longa linn* (*zingiberaceae*)	Rhizome mess	Acetone	curcumin	Randomized ed double bind placebo-controlled group design	53	4 w	Anti- bacterial and anti- inflammatory antioxidant	182
04	*Hemidesmus indicus* (*Apocynaceae*)	Roots	Ethanol	-	Randomize ed double bind placebo-controlled group design	53	4 w	Antibacterial and antimicrobial	182
05	*Garcinia mangostana* (*Guttiferae*)	Fruit	Hexane dichlorom ethane	xanthones	Randomized, phase3 double- blind, placebo controlled clinical trial	94	3w	Antimicrobial , anti- inflammatory, and antioxidants	183
06	*Butyrospermum paradoxum* (*sapotaceae*)	oil	Petroleum ether	saponin	A randomized comparative prospective blinded observational study	36	12weeks	Anti-bacterial	184
07	*Camellia sinensis* (*Theaceae*)	leaves	ethanol	Polyphenol ,polyunsatu rated fatty acid	A double- blind, randomized, controlled clinical trial	10	8weeks	5alpha reductase inhibitory anti-inflammatory	185
08	*Commiphora mukul* (*Burseraceae*)	Fruit	gugulipid	oleoresin	Randomized clinical trial	20	3 month hs	Anti-bacterial	186
09	*Hippophae rhamnoides* (*elaeagnaceae*)	Plant material	methanol	Vitamin c tocopherol	A single- blind, randomize d, placebo- controlled . split-face study.	50	12we eks	alpha reductase inhibitory	187
10	*Lenus culinaris (fabaceae)*	Powder	Acetic acid	Polyphenol polysaccharide ride flavonoid	Aprospective open non comparative phase 3 clinical trial	26	6w	Antioxidant anti-inflammatory anti-androgen anti-bacterial	188

Clinical review of Acane Vulgaris

11	*Vitex negundo (verbenaceae)*	plant	ethanol	Casticin isoorientin	Aprospective open non comparative phase 3 clinical trials	26	6W	Antioxidant anti-inflammatory anti-androgen anti-bacterial	188
12	*Cassia fistula*	leaves	methanol	Phenolic compound	A single- blind, randomize d, placebo- controlled , split-face study	50	12w	Antibacterial and anti- fungal	187
13	*Melaleuca alternifolia (myrtaceae)*	leaves	hexane	oil	A randomized ed double bind clinical trial	60	45 days	Anti-bacterial and anti- inflammatory activity	189
14	*Ocimum gratissimum (lamiaceae)*	leaf	hexane	Essential oil	Randomized clinical trial	84	4W	Anti-bacterial and anti-inflammatory	190
15	*Ocimum basilicum (lamiaceae)*	leaf	-	Essential oil	Randomized clinical trial	51	4W	Antibacterial activity	186
16	*Serenoa repens sesamum indicum (Arecaceae)*	Extract	-	Polyphenol argan oil	Clinical trial	20	4 weeks	Probably anti androgen activity	191
17	*Rhodomyrtus tomentosa (myrtle)*	leaf	ethanol	rhodomyrt one	randomiz ed and double-blind controlle d clinical trial	60	2w	Anti-bacterial	192
18	*Arographis paniculata (Acanthaceae)*	Leaf	ethanol	Polyphenol polysaccha ride and phenol	A prospecti ve, open, noncomp arative, phase III	26	6W	Antibacterial anti androgen and anti-inflammatory	188
19	*Salmalia malabarica (Malvaceae)*	seeds	Ethyl acetate	Polyphenol polysaccha ride, flavonoid	A prospective, open, noncomparative, phase III	26	6W	Anti-androgen anti-bacterial Anti-inflammatory antioxidant	188
20	*Nigella sativa (Butter cups)*	seeds	Ethyl acetate	Thymoquin one	randomized double- blind controlled clinical trial	60	2M	Anti- inflammatory and bacterial	193
21	*Terminalia arjuna (Combretaceae)*	Bark	Ethyl acetate hexane chlorofor m	Flavonoid and tannin	A randomized, double-blind, placebo- controlled parallel group	53	4W	Antibacterial anti inflammatory	182
22	*Ocimum gratissimum (Lamiaceae)*	Oil	Hexane	Essential oil	Blinding not stated, placebo- controlled RCT with 18 parallel	126	4W	Antibacterial	194
23	*Serenoa repens (Palms)*	Extract	Hexane	Polyphenol , argan oil	Clinical trial	20	4W	Anti-androgen	191

Clinical review of Acane Vulgaris

24	*Coleus forskohlii* (*Labiatae*)	Extract	methanol	Essential oil	randomized, double blind placebo- controlled clinical study	30	12W	Antibacterial	195
25	*Argania spinosa (Argan)*	oil	hexane	Argan oil poly phenol	Clinical trail	20	4W	Antiandrogen	191
26	*Allium cepa (Alliaceae)*	Bulb	Ethanol or water	Flavonoids	randomized, controlled, single- blind study	44	2W	Anti-Inflammatory	196
27	*Pterocarpus santalinus* (*Fabaceae*)	Leaves	Chloroform m and ethanol	Sesquiterpene	In vitro	45	4w	Anti-bacterial analgesic anti- inflammatory antioxidant	197
28	*Phyllanthus emblica* (*Phyllanthaceae*)	extract	Methanol acetone hexane	Tannin	randomize d, single- blind, placebo- controlled, split-face method	30	4w	Antioxidant anti sebum	198
29	*Zingiber cassumunar* (*Zingiberaceae*)	oil	Hexane	Terpinenes 4-ol	Four studies were randomized controlled trials	178	2M	Anti-bacterial	199
30	*Centella asiatica* (*Umbellifers*)	Leaf	Hexane ethyl acetate	Flavonoids hydroxybenzoic acid	A Split- Face, Double-Blind, Randomized, Placebo Controlled Trial	30	7D	Anti-bacterial anti inflammatory	200

Clinical review of Acane Vulgaris

CHAPTER V

Conclusion

In addition to screening phytocompounds (containing flavonoid, alkaloid, essential oils, phenol and phenolic compound, tannin, xanthone and xanthone derivatives, the bisnaphthquione derivative, diterpene acid, phenylpropanoid glycosides, acteoside, polyunsaturated fatty acid, etc.), developing an appropriate delivery system that imparts their efficacies and avoids irritation or allergy in patients with hypersensitive skin can play an imperative role in safety and efficacy of them. Besides, combination treatment also should be used to find more effective agent with regard to synergistic effects on the pathogenesis of acne. Much disparate and introductory research exists on the effects of herbs on multiple aspects of acne. A comprehensive approach combining multiple herbs as well as lifestyle and dietary changes has helped people with acne in preliminary clinical trials. The continued resistance of mainstream dermatology to the possibility of this approach does not optimally serve patients who might be significantly helped by natural therapies. There are sufficient pilot data to warrant larger trials on various herbal medicines in isolation and combined with each other and other natural therapies. The data are also sufficient to support a recommendation for use of these herbs in clinical practice. This is particularly true, given how safe they are. Overall, herbal medicine has much to offer to improve our ability to deal with the complex issues acne presents.

References

1. White, G. M. Recent findings in the epidemiologic evidence, classification, and subtypes of acne vulgaris. J. Am. Acad. Dermatol. 39, S34–S37 (1998).
2. Vos, T. et al. Years lived with disability (YLDs) for 1160 sequelae of 289 diseases and injuries 1990–2010: a systematic analysis for the Global Burden of Disease study 2010. Lancet 380, 2163–2196 (2012).
3. Gollnick, H. P. & Finlay, A. Y., Shear, N. & Global Alliance to Improve Outcomes in Acne. Can we define acne as a chronic disease? If so, how and when? Am. J. Clin. Dermatol. 9, 279–284 (2008). An important article suggesting the chronic nature of acne.
4. Jowett S, Ryan T. Skin disease and handicap: an analysis of the impact of skin conditions. Soc Sci Med 1985; 20: 425–29.
5. Gupta MA, Gupta AK. Depression and suicidal ideation in dermatology patients with acne, alopecia areata, atopic dermatitis and psoriasis. Br J Dermatol 1998; 139: 846– 50.
6. Cotterill JA, Cunliffe WJ. Suicide in dermatological patients. Br J Dermatol 1997; 137: 246–50.
7. Cunliffe WJ. Unemployment and acne. Br J Dermatol 1986; 115: 386.
8. Norris JF, Cunliffe WJ. A histological and immunocytochemical study of early acne lesions. Br J Dermatol 1988; 118: 651–59.
9. Mouser PE, Baker BS, Seaton ED, Chu AC. Propionibacterium acnes reactive Th-1 cells in the skin cross-sectional study protocol. Medicine (Baltimore). 2017; 96(45):e8554.
10. Leyden JL, McGinley KJ, Mills OH, Kligman AM. Propionibacterium levels in patients with and without acne vulgaris. J Invest Dermatol 1975; 65: 382–84.
11. Eady EA, Jones CE, Tipper JL, Cove JH, Cunliffe WJ, Layton AM. Antibiotic resistant propionibacteria in acne: need for policies to modify antibiotic usage. BMJ 1993; 306: 555–56.
12. Toyoda M, Morohashi M. Pathogenesis of acne. Med Electron Microsc 2001;34:29– 40.
13. Gollnick H, Cunliffe W, Berson D, Dreno B, Finlay A, Leyden JJ, et al. Management of acne: a report from a global alliance to improve outcomes in acne. J Am Acad Dermatol 2003;49:1–37.

1. Kanlayavattanakul M, Lourith N. Therapeutic agents and herbs in topical application for acne treatment. Int J Cosmet Sci 2011;33:289–97.
2. Feldman S, Careccia RE, Barham KL, Hancox J. Diagnosis and treatment of acne. Am Fam Physician 2004;69:2123–30.
3. Titus S, Hodge J. Diagnosis and treatment of acne. Am Fam Physician. 2012;86(8):734-740. Accessed July 11, 2019. https://www.aafp.org/ afp/2012/1015/p734.html
4. Kim K, Ha I, Kim E, et al. A comparative study of biological and metabolic biomarkers between healthy individuals and patients with acne vulgaris: af patients with acne vulgaris. J Invest Dermatol (in press).
5. Coates P, Vyakarnam S, Eady EA, et al. Prevalence of antibiotic-resistant propionibacteria on the skin of acne patients: 10-year surveillance data and snapshot distribution study. Br J Dermatol 2002;146:840–848.
6. Eady EA, Gloor M, Leyden JJ. Propionibacterium acnes resistance: A worldwide problem. Dermatology 2003;206:54–56.
7. Honein MA, Paulozzi LJ, Erickson JD. Continued occurrence of Accutane-exposed pregnancies. Teratology 2001;64:142–147.
8. Magin PJ, Adams J, Pond CD, Smith W. Topical and oral CAM in acne: A review of the empirical evidence and a consideration of its context. Complement Ther Med 2006:14:62–76
9. As city immigration thrives, diversity bounds. The New York Times. November 8, 1999; Metropolitan Desk Section.
10. Fox H. Observations on skin diseases in the Negro. J Cutan Dis 1908;26:67-79.

11. Hazen H. Personal observations upon skin diseases in the American Negro. J Cutan Dis 1914;32:704-6.

12. Kenney JA. Management of dermatoses peculiar to Negroes. Arch Dermatol 1965;91:126-9.

13. Halder RM, Grimes PE, McLaurin CL, Kress MA, Kenney JA Jr. Incidence of common dermatoses in pupils: a community-based study. J Invest Dermatol 2009; 129: 2136–41.

14. Child FJ, Fuller LC, Higgins EM, Du Vivier AWP. A study of the spectrum of skin disease occurring in a black population in south-east London. Br J Dermatol 1999;141:512-7.

28. Goh CL, Akarapanth R. Epidemiology of skin disease among children in a referral skin clinic in Singapore. Pediatr Dermatol 1994;11(2):125-8.

29. Nanda A, Al-Hasawi F, Alsaleh QA. A prospective survey of pediatric dermatology clinic patients in Kuwait: an analysis of 10,000 cases. Pediatr Dermatol 1999;16(1):6- 11.

30. Schachner L, Ling NS, Press S. A statistical analysis of a pediatric dermatology clinic. Pediatr Dermatol 1983;1(2):157-64.

31. Strauss JS, Thiboutot DM. Diseases of the sebaceous glands. In: Freedberg IM, Eisen AZ, Wolff K, et al, editors. Fitzpatrick's dermatology in general medicine. Vol 1. New York: McGraw-Hill; 1999. p. 769-84.

32. Lucky AW. A review of infantile and pediatric acne. Dermatology 1998; 196: 95–97.

33. Law MP, Chuh AA, Lee A, Molinari N. Acne prevalence and beyond: acne disability and its predominantly black dermatologic practice. Cutis 1983;32:388-90.

34. .Ghodsi SZ, Orawa H, Zouboulis CC. Prevalence, severity, and severity risk factors of acne in high school

35. Stathakis V, Kilkenny M, Marks R. Descriptive epidemiology of acne vulgaris in the community. Australas J Dermatol 1997; 38: 115–23.

36. Menon C, Gipson K, Bowe WP, Hoff stad OJ, Margolis DJ. Validity of subject self- report for acne. Dermatology 2008; 217: 164–68

37. Collier CN, Harper JC, Cafardi JA, et al. The prevalence of acne in adults 20 years and older. J Am Acad Dermatol 2008; 58: 56–59.

38. Poli F, Dreno B, Verschoore M. An epidemiological study of acne in female adults: results of a survey conducted in France. J Eur Acad Dermatol Venereol 2001; 15: 541–45.

39. Schafer T, Nienhaus A, Vieluf D, Berger J, Ring J. Epidemiology of acne in the general population: the risk of smoking. Br J Dermatol 2001; 145: 100–104.

40. Cunliffe WJ, Gould DJ. Prevalence of facial acne vulgaris in late adolescence and in adults. BMJ 1979; 1: 1109–10.

41. Friedlander SF, Eichenfi eld LF, Fowler JF Jr, Fried RG, Levy ML, Webster GF. Acne epidemiology and pathophysiology. Semin Cutan Med Surg 2010; 29: 2–4

42. Mourelatos K, Eady EA, Cunliffe WJ, Clark SM, Cove JH. Temporal changes in sebum excretion and propionibacterium colonization in preadolescent children with and without acne. Br J Dermatol 2007; 156: 22–31

43. Stoll S, Shalita AR, Webster GF, Kaplan R, Danesh S, Penstein A. The effect of the menstrual cycle on acne. J Am Acad Dermatol 2001; 45: 957–60.

44. Yosipovitch G, Tang M, Dawn AG, et al. Study of psychological stress, sebum production and acne vulgaris in adolescents. Acta Derm Venereol 2007; 87: 135–39.

45. Cheng CE, Irwin B, Mauriello D, Liang L, Pappert A, Kimball AB. Self-reported acne severity, treatment, and belief patterns across multiple racial and ethnic groups in adolescent students. Pediatr Dermatol 2010; 27: 446–52.

46. Gollnick HP, Finlay AY, Shear N. Global alliance to improve outcomes in acne. Can we define acne as a chronic disease? If so, how and when? Am J Clin Dermatol 2008; 9: 279–84.pubertal maturation and age. Arch Dermatol 1991; 127:210–16.

47. Thiboutot D, Gollnick H, Bettoli V, et al. Global Alliance to Improve Outcomes in Acne. New insights into the management of acne: an update from the Global Alliance to Improve Outcomes in Acne group. J Am Acad Dermatol 2009; 60: S1–50.

48. Downie MM, Sanders DA, Kealey T. Modelling the remission of individual acne lesions in vitro. Br J Dermatol

2002; 147: 869–78.

49. Cunliffe WJ, Shuster S. Pathogenesis of acne. Lancet 1969; ii: 685–87.results of a five-year longitudinal study. J Pediatr 1997; 130:30–9.

50. Seirafi H, Farnaghi F, Vasheghani-Farahani A, et al. Assessment of androgens in women with adult-onset acne. Int J Dermatol 2007; 46: 1188–91.

51. Law MPM, Chuh AAT, Molinari N, Lee A. Acne prevalence and beyond: acne disability and its predictive factors among Chinese late adolescents in Hong Kong. Clin Exp Dermatol 2010; 35:16–21 [erratum in Clin Exp Dermatol 2010; 35:339].

52. Yahya H. Acne vulgaris in Nigerian adolescents: prevalence, severity, beliefs, perceptions, and practices. Int J Dermatol 2009; 48:498–505.

53. Rademaker M, Garioch JJ, Simpson NB. Acne in schoolchildren: no longer a concern for dermatologists. BMJ 1989; 298:1217–19.

54. Lucky AW. A review of infantile and pediatric acne. Dermatology 1998; 196:95–7.

55. Wei B, Pang Y, Qu L et al. The epidemiology of adolescent acne in North East China. J Eur Acad Dermatol Venereol 2010; 24:953–74.

56. Kraning KK, Odland GF. Prevalence, morbidity and cost of dermatologic diseases. J Invest Dermatol 1979; 73:395–401.

57. White GM. Recent findings in the epidemiologic evidence, classification, and subtypes of acne vulgaris. J Am Acad Dermatol 1998; 39:S34–7.

58. Lucky AW, Biro FM, Huster GA et al. Acne vulgaris in early adolescent boys: correlations with

59. Lucky AW, Biro FM, Simbart LA et al. Predictors of severity of acne vulgaris in young adolescent girls: chronic disease? If so, how and when? Am J Clin Dermatol 2008; 9:279–84.

60. Rea JN, Newhouse ML, Halil T. Skin disease in Lambeth. A community study of prevalence and use of medical care. Br J Prev Soc Med 1976; 30:107–14

61. Wolkenstein P, Grob JJ, Bastuji-Garin S et al. French people and skin diseases: results of a survey using a representative sample. Arch Dermatol 2003; 139:1614–19.

62. Johnson MT, Roberts J. Skin conditions and related need for medical care among persons 1–74 years. United States, 1971– 1974. Vital Health Stat 11 1978; 212:i–v, 1–

72.

63. Williams HC, Dellavalle RP, Garner S. Acne vulgaris. Lancet 2011; 379:361–72.

64. Friedlander SF, Eichenfield LF, Fowler JF Jr et al. Acne epidemiology and pathophysiology. Semin Cutan Med Surg 2010; 29 (2 Suppl. 1):2–4.

65. Mancini AJ, Baldwin HE, Eichenfield LF et al. Acne life cycle: the spectrum of pediatric disease. Semin Cutan Med Surg 2011; 30 (3 Suppl.):S2–5.

66. Sorensen K, Aksglaede L, Petersen JH, Juul A. Recent changes in pubertal timing in healthy Danish boys: associations with body mass index. J Clin Endocrinol Metab 2010; 95:263–70.

67. Gollnick HP, Finlay AY, Shear N. Global alliance to improve outcomes in acne. Can we define acne as a

68. Poli F, Dreno B, Verschoore M. An epidemiological study of acne in female adults: results of a survey conducted in France. J Eur Acad Dermatol Venereol 2001; 15:541– 5.

69. Collier CN, Harper JC, Cafardi JA et al. The prevalence of acne in adults 20 years and older. J Am Acad Dermatol 2008; 58:56–9.

70. Thiboutot D, Gollnick H, Bettoli V et al. New insights into the management of acne: an update from the Global Alliance to Improve Outcomes in Acne group. J Am Acad Dermatol 2009; 60 (5 Suppl.):S1–50.

71. Schafer T, Nienhaus A, Vieluf D et al. Epidemiology of acne in the general population: the risk of smoking. Br J

Dermatol 2001; 145:100–4.

72. Cunliffe WJ, Gould DJ. Prevalence of facial acne vulgaris in late adolescence and in adults. BMJ Case Rep 1979; 1:1109–10.
73. Stathakis V, Kilkenny M, Marks R. Descriptive epidemiology of acne vulgaris in the community. Australas J Dermatol 1997; 38:115–23.
74. Ghodsi SZ, Orawa H, Zouboulis CC. Prevalence, severity, and severity risk factors of acne in high school pupils: a community based study. J Invest Dermatol 2009; 129:2136–41.
75. Krowchuk DP. Managing acne in adolescents. Pediatr Clin North Am 2000; 47:841– 57.
76. Lee SH, Cho HS, Seung NR et al. Quality of life of acne patients. Korean J Dermatol 2006; 44:688–95.
77. Dunn LK, O'Neill JL, Feldman SR. Acne in adolescents: quality of life, self-esteem, mood, and psychological disorders. Dermatol Online J 2011; 17:1.
78. Tan JKL, Li Y, Fung K et al. Divergence of demographic factors associated with clinical severity compared with quality of life impact in acne. J Cutan Med Surg 2008; 12:235–42.
79. Jones-Caballero M, Chren MM, Soler B et al. Quality of life in mild to moderate acne: relationship to clinical severity and factors influencing change with treatment. J Eur Acad Dermatol Venereol 2007; 21:219–26.
80. Maguire K, Westhoff C. The state of hormonal contraception today: established and emerging noncontraceptive health benefits. Am J Obstet Gynecol 2011; 205 (4 Suppl.):S4–8.
81. Kubota Y, Shirahige Y, Nakai K et al. Community-based epidemiological study of psychosocial effects of acne in Japanese adolescents. J Dermatol 2010; 37:617–22.
82. Aktan S, Ozmen E, Sanli B. Anxiety, depression, and nature of acne vulgaris in adolescents. Int J Dermatol 2000; 39:354–7.
83. Dalgard F, Svensson A, Holm JO, Sundby J. Self-reported skin morbidity in Oslo. Associations with sociodemographic factors among adults in a cross-sectional study. Br J Dermatol 2004; 151:452–7.
84. Magin P, Adams J, Heading G, Pond D. 'Perfect skin', the media and patients with skin disease: a qualitative study of patients with acne, psoriasis and atopic eczema. Aust J Prim Health 2011; 17:181–5.

85. Halvorsen JA, Stern RS, Dalgard F et al. Suicidal ideation, mental health problems, and social impairment are increased in adolescents with acne: a population-based study. J Invest Dermatol 2011; 131:363–70.
86. Magin P, Adams J, Heading G, Pond D. Acne's relationship with psychiatric and psychological morbidity: results of a school-based cohort study of adolescents. J Eur Acad Dermatol Venereol 2010; 24:58–64.
87. Kokandi A. Evaluation of acne quality of life and clinical severity in acne female adults. Dermatol Res Pract 2010; 2010:410809.
88. Kurtalic N, Hadzijahic N, Tahirovic H, Sigercic N. [Quality-of life of adolescents with acne vulgaris]. Acta Med Croatica 2010; 64:247–51 (in Croatian).
89. Hanisah A, Omar K, Shah SA. Prevalence of acne and its impact on the quality of life in school-aged adolescents in Malaysia. J Prim Health Care 2009; 1:20–5.
90. Krejci-Manwaring J, Schulz MR, Feldman SR et al. Social sensitivity and acne: the role of personality in negative social consequences and quality of life. Int J Psychiatry Med 2006; 91.:121–30. 2012 The Authors BJD 2012 British Association of

Dermatologists 2013 168, pp 474–485 482 Epidemiology of acne vulgaris, K. Bhate and H.C. Williams.

91. Al Robaee AA. Assessment of general health and quality of life in patients with acne using a validated generic questionnaire. Acta Dermatovenerol Alp Panonica Adriat 2009; 18:157–64.
92. Magin PJ, Pond CD, Smith WT et al. A cross-sectional study of psychological morbidity in patients with acne, psoriasis and atopic dermatitis in specialist dermatology and general practices. J Eur Acad Dermatol Venereol 2008; 22:1435–44.

93. Diamantis SS, Waldorf HA. Rosacea: clinical presentation and pathophysiology. J Drugs Dermatol 2006; 5:8–12.

94. Antoniou C, Dessinioti C, Stratigos AJ, Katsambas AD. Clinical and therapeutic approach to childhood acne: an update. Pediatr Dermatol 2009; 26:373–80.

95. Ingram JRJ. The aetiology of acne inversa: an evolving story. Br J Dermatol 2011; 165:231–2.

96. Vos, T. et al. Years lived with disability (YLDs) for 1160 sequelae of 289 diseases and injuries 1990–2010: a systematic analysis for the Global Burden of Disease Study 2010. The Lancet. 380(9859), 2163–96, https://doi.org/10.1016/s0140-

6736(12)61729-2 (2012).

97. Stathakis, V., Kilkenny, M. & Marks, R. Descriptive epidemiology of acne vulgaris in the community. Australas J Dermatol. 38(3), 115–23, https://doi.org/10.1111/j.1440- 0960.1997.tb01126.x (1997)

98. Seattle WI. *GBD Compare.* Seattle: University of Washington; 2013.

99. Quarles FN, Johnson BA, Badreshia S, et al. Acne vulgaris in richly pigmented patients. *Dermatol Ther.* 2007;20(3):122–127.

100. Davis EC, Callender VD. A review of acne in ethnic skin: pathogenesis, clinical manifestations, and management strategies. *J Clin Aesthet Dermatol.* 2010;3(4):24– 38.

101. Pochi PE, Strauss JS. Sebaceous gland activity in black skin. *Dermatol Clin.*

1988;6(3):349–3

102. Grimes P, Edison BL, Green BAY, Wildnauer RH. Evaluation of inherent differences between African American and white skin surface properties using subjective and objective measures. *Cutis.* 2004;73(6):392–396.

103. Bagatin E, Timpano DL, Guadanhim LR, et al. Acne vulgaris: prevalence and clinical forms in adolescents from Sao Paulo, Brazil. *An Bras Dermatol.* 2014;89(3):428–435.

104. Perkins AC, Cheng CE, Hillebrand GG, Miyamoto K, Kimball AB. Comparison of the epidemiology of acne vulgaris among Caucasian, Asian, Continental Indian and African American women. *J Eur Acad Dermatol Venereol.* 2011;25(9):1054–1060. related treatment of acne. J Dermatol 1991;18(9):489-99.

105. Halder RM, Nootheti PK. Ethnic skin disorders overview. *J Am Acad Dermatol.*

2003;48(6 Suppl):S143–S148.

106. Callender VD. Acne in ethnic skin: special considerations for therapy. *Dermatol Ther.*

2004;17(2):184–195.

107. Friedman HL. The health of adolescents: beliefs and behaviour. *Soc Sci Med.*

1989;29(3):309–315.

108. Magin P, Pond D, Smith W, Watson A. A systematic review of the evidence for 'myths and misconceptions' in acne management: diet,face-washing and sunlight. *Fam Pract.* 2005;22(1):62–70.

109. Plewig G, Fulton JE, Kligman AM. Pomade acne. *Arch Dermatol.* 1970;101(5):580– 584.

110. Lobo RA. Hirsutism, alopecia, and acne. In: Becker KL, Bilezikian JP, eds. Principles and Practice of Endocrinology and Metabolism. 2nd ed. Philadelphia, Pa: JB Lippincott Williams & Wilkins; 1995:924-940.

111. Webster GF. Acne vulgaris: state of the science. Arch Dermatol. 1999;135:1101- 1102.

112. Thiboutot D. Hormones and acne: pathophysiology, clinical evaluation, and therapies. Semin Cutan Med Surg.

2001;20:144-153.

113. Akimoto N, Sato T, Sakiguchi T, et al. Cell proliferation and lipid formation in hamster sebaceous gland cells. Dermatology. 2002;204:118-123.

114. Gollnick HP, Zouboulis CC, Akamatsu H, Kurokawa I, Schulte A. Pathogenesis and pathogenesis dependent skin disorders. Dermatology 1996;193(3):177-84.

115. Harris HH, Downing DT, Stewart ME, Strauss JS. Sustainable rates of sebum secretion in acne patients and matched normal control subjects. J Am Acad Dermatol 1983;8(2):200-3.

116. .Blauer M, Vaalasti A, Pauli SL, Ylikomi T, Joensuu T, Tuohimaa P. Location of androgen receptor in human skin. J Invest Dermatol 1991;97(2):264-8.

117. Choudhry R, Hodgins MB, Van der Kwast TH, Brinkmann AO, Boersma WJ. Localization of androgen receptors in human skin by immunohistochemistry: Implications for the hormonal regulation of hair growth, sebaceous glands and sweat glands. J Endocrinol 1992;133(3):467-75.

118. Thigpen AE, Silver RI, Guileyardo JM, Casey ML, McConnell JD, Russell DW. Tissue distribution and ontogeny of steroid 5a-reductase isozyme expression. J Clin Invest 1993;92(2):903-10.

119. Luu-The V, Sugimoto Y, Puy L, Labrie Y, Lopez-Solache I, Singh M, et al. Characterization, expression, and immunohistochemical localization of 5-a-reductase in human skin. J Invest Dermatol 1994;102(2):221-6.

120. Thiboutot D, Harris G, Iles V, Cimis G, Gilliland K, Hagari S. Activity of the type I 5 a-reductase exhibits regional differences in isolated sebaceous glands and whole skin. J Invest Dermatol 1995;105(2):209-14.

121. Chen W, Zouboulis CC, Orfanos CE. The 5 a reductase system and its inhibitors: Recent development and its perspective in treating androgen Modlin RL. Activation of toll-like receptor 2 in acne triggers inflammatory cytokine responses. J Immunol 2002; 169: 1535–1541.

122. Zouboulis CC, Seltmann H, Hiroi N, Chen W, Young M, Oeff M, et al. Corticotropin- releasing hormone: An autocrine hormone that promotes lipogenesis in human sebocytes. Proc Natl Acad Sci U S A 2002;99(10):7148-53.

123. Orth DN, Kovacs WJ. The adrenal cortex. In: Wilson JD, Foster DW, Kronenberg HM, Larsen PR, editors. Williams Textbook of Endocrinology. Philadelphia, PA: WB. Saunders; 1998. p. 517-664.

124. Zouboulis CC, Xia L, Akamatsu H, Seltmann H, Fritsch M, Hornemann S, et al. The human sebocyte culture model provides new insights into development and management of seborrhoea and acne. Dermatology 1998;196(1):21-31.

125. Zouboulis CC, Xia L, Akamatsu H, Seltmann H, Hornemann S, Rühl R, Chen W, Nau H, Orfanos CE. The human sebocyte culture model provides insights into development and management of seborrhea and acne. Dermatol 1998; 196: 21–31.

126. GuyR, Green MR,Kealey. Modeling acne in vitro.JInvest Dermatol 1996; 106: 176–

182.

127. Downing DT, Stewart ME, Wertz PW, Strauss JS. Essential fatty acids and acne. J Am Acad Dermatol 1986;14:221-5.

128. Zouboulis C. Update on sebaceous gland physiology: Induction of inflammation and its clinical implications. JEADV 2001;15 Suppl 2:102.

129. Kim J, Ochoa MT,Krutzik SR,Takeuchi O, Uematsu S, Legaspi AJ, Brightbill HD, Holland D, Cunliffe WJ, Akira S, Sieling PA, Godowski PJ,.online ahead of print May 28, 2019]. J Dermatolog Treat. doi:10.1080/09546634.2019.1618434.

130. Zouboulis CC, Nestoris S, Adler YD, Orth M, Orfanos CE, Picardo M, Camera E, Cunliffe WJ. A new concept for acne therapy: a pilot study with zileuton, an oral 5- lipoxygenase inhibitor. Arch Dermatol 2003; 139: 668–670.

131. Kirschbaum JO, Kligman AM. The pathogenic role of Corynebacterium acnes in acne vulgaris. Arch Dermatol 1963;88:832-3.

132. Marples RR, McGinley KJ. Corynebacterium acnes and other anaerobic diphtheroids from human skin. J Med

Microbiol 1974;7(3):349-57.

133. Witkowski JA, Parish LC. The assessment of acne: An evaluation of grading and lesion counting in the measurement of acne. Clin Dermatol 2004;22:394-7.

134. Witkowski JA, Parish LC. From the ghosts of the past: Acne lesion counting. J Am Acad Dermatol 1999;40:131.

135. Moradi Tuchayi S, Alexander TM, Nadkarni A, Feldman SR. Interventions to increase adherence to acne treatment. Patient Prefer Adherence. 2016;10:2091–2096

136. Hayran Y, _ Incel Uysal P, Öktem A, Aksoy GG, Akdogan N, Yalçın B. Factors affecting adherence and patient satisfaction with treatment: a cross sectional study of 500 patients with acne vulgaris [published adapalene 0.3%/benzoyl peroxide 2.5% gel in subjects with moderate or severe facial acne: results of a 6-month randomized, vehicle-controlled trial using intraindividual comparison. Am J Clin Dermatol. 2018;19(2):275–286.

137. Anderson KL, Dothard EH, Huang KE, Feldman SR. Frequency of primary nonadherence to acne treatment. JAMA Dermatol. 2015;151(6):623–626

138. Zaenglein AL, Pathy AL, Schlosser BJ, et al. Guidelines of care for the management of acne vulgaris. J Am Acad Dermatol. 2016;74(5):945–973.e33.

139. Ryskina KL, Goldberg E, Lott B, Hermann D, Barbieri JS, Lipoff JB. The role of the physician in patient perceptions of barriers to primary adherence with acne medications. JAMA Dermatol. 2018;154(4):456–459.

140. Boker A, Feetham HJ, Armstrong A, Purcell P, Jacobe H. Do automated text messages increase adherence to acne therapy? Results of a randomized, controlled trial. J Am Acad Dermatol. 2012;67(6):1136–1142.

141. Leyden J, Stein-Gold L, Weiss J. Why topical retinoids are the mainstay of therapy for acne. Dermatol Ther (Heidelb). 2017;7(3):293–304.

142. Leyden JJ, Shalita A, Thiboutot D, Washenik K, Webster G. Topical retinoids in inflammatory acne: a retrospective, investigator-blinded, vehicle-controlled, photographic assessment. Clin Ther. 2005;27(2): 216–224.

143. Dréno B, Bissonnette R, Gagné-Henley A, et al. Prevention and reduction of atrophic acne scars with

144. Thiboutot DM, Dréno B, Abanmi A, et al. Practical management of acne for clinicians: an international consensus from the Global Alliance to Improve Outcomes in Acne. J Am Acad Dermatol. 2018;78(2 suppl 1):S1–S23.e1.

145. Zaenglein AL, Pathy AL, Schlosser BJ, et al. Guidelines of care for the management of acne vulgaris. J Am Acad Dermatol. 2016;74(5):945–973.e33.

146. Walsh TR, Efthimiou J, Dréno B. Systematic review of antibiotic resistance in acne: an increasing topical and oral threat. Lancet Infect Dis. 2016;16(3):e23–e33.

147. Adler BL, Kornmehl H, Armstrong AW. Antibiotic resistance in acne treatment. JAMA Dermatol. 2017;153(8):810–811.

148. Cunliffe WJ, Holland KT, Bojar R, Levy SF. A randomized, double-blind comparison of a clindamycin phosphate/benzoyl peroxide gel formulation and a matching clindamycin gel with respect to microbiologic activity and clinical efficacy in the topical treatment of acne vulgaris. Clin Ther. 2002;24(7): 1117–1133.

149. Ross JI, Snelling AM, Carnegie E, et al. Antibiotic-resistant acne: lessons from Europe. Br J Dermatol. 2003;148(3): 467–478.

150. Simonart T, Dramaix M. Treatment of acne with topical antibiotics: lessons from clinical studies. Br J Dermatol. 2005;153(2):395–403.

151. Fanelli M, Kupperman E, Lautenbach E, Edelstein PH, Margolis DJ. Antibiotics, acne, and Staphylococcus aureus colonization. Arch Dermatol. 2011; 147(8):917–921.

152. Dutil M. Benzoyl peroxide: enhancing antibiotic efficacy in acne management. Skin Therapy Lett. 2010;15(10):5–7.

153. US Food and Drug Administration. Drug approval package: Seysara (sarecycline). 2018. Available at: https://www.accessdata.fda.gov/drugsatfda_ docs/nda/2018/209521Orig1s000TOC. cfm. Accessed April 5, 2019.

154. Andriessen A, Lynde CW. Antibiotic resistance: shifting the paradigm in topical acne treatment. J Drugs Dermatol. 2014;13(11):1358–1364.

155. Tan JK, Ediriweera C. Efficacy and safety of combined ethinyl estradiol/drospirenone oral contraceptives in the treatment of acne. Int J Womens Health 2010: 1: 213–221.

156. Danby FW. Acne and milk, the diet myth, and beyond. J Am Acad Dermatol. 2005;52:360–2.

157. Arora M, Yadav A, Saini V. Role of hormones in acne vulgaris. Clin Biochem. 2011;44:1035–40. [PubMed] [Google Scholar]

158. Melnik BC. Milk – the promoter of chronic Western diseases. Med Hypoth. 2009;72:631–9.

159. Bowe WP, Joshi SS, Shalita AR. Diet and acne. J Am Acad Dermatol. 2010;63:124– 41.

160. Adilson C, Thais Abdalla M. Acne and diet: truth or myth? An Bras Dermatol. 2010;85:346–53

161. Block SG, Valins WE, Caperton CV, et al. Exacerbation of facial acne vulgaris after consuming pure chocolate. *J Am Acad Dermatol.* 2011;65:e114–5.

162. Emiroğlu N, Cengiz FP, Kemeriz F. Insulin resistance in severe acne vulgaris. *Postep Derm Alergol.* 2015;32:281–5.

163. Kaufman WH. The diet and acne. Arch Dermatol. 1983;119:276.

164. Smith RN, Mann NJ, Braue A, et al. A low-glycemic-load diet improves symptoms in acne vulgaris patients: a randomized controlled trial. Am J Clin Nutr. 2007;86:107– 15.

165. Bowe WP, Joshi SS, Shalita AR. Diet and acne. J Am Acad Dermatol. 2010;63:124– 41

166. Bowe WP, Shalita AR. Effective over-the-counter acne treatments. Semin Cutan Med Surg. 2008;27:170–6.

167. Gawęcki J. *Podstawy nauki o żywieniu.* Warsaw: Wyd. Naukowe PWN; 2012. Żywienie człowieka.

168. Von Tappeiner H, Jodlbauer A. Uber die wirkung der photodynamischen (fluoreszierenden) stoffe auf protozoen und enzyme. Dtsch Arch Klin Med 1904;80:427–87.

169. Passow A, Rimpau W. Untersuchungen uber photodynamische wirkungen auf bakterien. Munch Med Wochenschr 1924;23:733–7.

170. Meffert H, Gaunitz K, Gutewort T, Amlong UJ. Therapy of acne with visible light: decreased irradiation time by using a blue-light high energy lamp. Dermatol Monatsschr 1990;176:597–603.

171. Sigurdsson V, Knulst AC, van Weelden H. Phototherapy of acne vulgaris with visible light. Dermatology 1997;94:256–60.

172. Anna Hwee Sing Heng & Fook Tim Chew Systematic review of the epidemiology of acne vulgari 5754 (2020) .

173. Kaiane A. Habeshian, MD;Bernard A. Cohen, MDcurrent Issues in the Treatment of Acne Vulgaris MAY 01 2020.

174. Tian-Xin Cong, Dan Hao, Xiang Wen, Xiao-Hua Li, Gu He & Xian Jiang From pathogenesis of acne vulgaris to anti-acne agents 337–349 (2019).

175. Husein Husein-ElAhmed Management of acne vulgaris with hormonal therapies in adult female patients 06 April 2015.

176. Sara Moradi Tuchayi, Evgenia Makrantonaki, Ruta Gancevicene, Clio Dessinioti, Steven R. Feldman & Christos C. Zouboulis Acne vulgaris 15029 (2015).

177. Bodo C Melnik Linking diet to acne metabolomics, inflammation, and comedogenesis: an update 2015; 8: 371–388.

178. Manoj A. Suva1 *, Ankita M. Patel2 , Neeraj Sharma1 , Chandrayee Bhattacharya1 , Ravi K. Mangi1 A Brief Review on Acne Vulgaris: Pathogenesis, Diagnosis and Treatment ISSN: 2230-9861 (online), ISSN: 2349-1299 (print) Volume 4, Issue 3.

179. HaniehAzimiMehrnazFallah-TaftiAli AsgharKhakshurMohammadAbdollahi A review of phytotherapy of acne vulgaris: Perspective of new pharmacological treatments Volume 83, Issue 8, December 2012.

180. Hywel C Williams, Robert P Dellavalle, Sarah Garner Acne vulgaris Lancet 2012; 379: 361–72.

181. Sanjay K Rathi ACNE VULGARIS TREATMENT : THE CURRENT SCENARIO 2011 Jan-Feb; 56(1): 7–13.

182. Lalla JK, Nandedkar SY, Paranjape MH, Talreja NB. Clinical trials of ayurvedic formulations in the treatment of acne vulgaris. J Ethnopharmacol 2001;78:99–102.

183. Toni Sutono Efficacy of Garcinia mangostana L. (mangosteen rind extract) to reduce acne severity 22(3):167.

184. Alebiosu CO, Ogun Laduma, Ogunleye DS. A report of a clinical trial conducted on Toto ointment and soap products. J Natl Med Assoc 2003;95: 95–105.

185. Mahmood T, Akhtar N, Khan BA, Khan HM, Saeed T. Outcomes of 3% green tea emulsion on skin sebum production in male volunteers. Bosn J Basic Med Sci 2010;10:260–4.

186. Magin PJ, Adams J, Pond CD, Smith W. Topical and oral CAM in acne: a review of the empirical evidence and a consideration of its context. Complement Ther Med 2006;14:62–76.

187. Barkat Ali Khancorresponding author and Naveed Akhtar Clinical and sebumetric evaluation of topical emulsions in the treatment of acne vulgaris 2014 Aug; 31(4): 229–234.

188. Ravichandran G, Bharadwaj VS. Evaluation of efficacy and safety of Acne-N-Pimple cream in acne vulgaris. Antiseptic 2004;101:249–55.

189. Ensieh S, Jooya A, Siadat AH, Iraji F. The efficacy of 5% topical tea tree oil gel in mild to moderate acne vulgaris: a randomized, double-blind placebo-controlled study. Indian J Dermatol Venereol Leprol 2007;73: 22–5.

190. Orafidiya LO, Agabani EO, Oyedele AO, Babalola OO, Onayemi O, Aiyedun FF. The effect of aloe vera gel on the anti-acne properties of the essential oil of Ocimum gratissimum Linn leaf — a preliminary clinical investigation. Int J Aromather 2004;14:15–21.

191. Dobrev H. Clinical and instrumental study of the efficacy of a new sebum control cream. J Cosmet Dermatol 2007;6:113–8.

192. Suttiwan Wunnoo, Siwaporn Bilhman, Thanaporn Amnuaikit, Julalak C Ontong, Sudarshan Singh, Sauvarat Au Pemkiate, Supayang P VoravuthikunchaiRhodomyrtone as a New Natural Antibiotic Isolated from Rhodomyrtus tomentosa Leaf Extract: A Clinical Application in the Management of Acne Vulgaris 2021 Jan 22;10(2).

193. SamanSoleymani,ArmanZargaran,MohammadHoseinFarzaei,AminIranpanah,Fateme hHeydarpour,Fariba Najafi,Roja RahimiThe effect of a hydrogel made by Nigella sativa L. on acne vulgaris: A randomized double-blind clinical trial17 June 2020.

194. Martin KW, Ernst E. Herbal medicines for treatment of bacterialinfections: a review of controlled clinical trials. J Antimicrob Chemother2003;51:241–6.

195. The Effect of Coleus Forskohlii Extract on the Risk Factors of Metabolic SyndromeClinicalTrials.gov Identifier: NCT02143349.

196. Zoe D. Draelos,Leslie Baumann,b Alan B. Fleischer, JR.,,c Stefan Plaum,c Edward V. Avakian,corresponding author and Bhushan Hardas, A New Proprietary Onion Extract Gel Improves the Appearance of New Scars2012 June; 5(6).

197. Dinesh Kumar Anti-inflammatory, analgesic, and antioxidant activities of methanolic wood extract of Pterocarpus santalinus L. PMC3157138.

198. 185.Thanaroat,Timudom,Chaiyavat,Chaiyasut,ORCID,Bhagavathi,Sundaramivamarut hORCID,Pratyay Tiampasook 1 andDuangporn Nacapunchai ,Anti-Sebum Efficacy of Phyllanthus emblica L. (Emblica) Toner on Facial Skin 2020, *10*(22).

199. Bunchai Chongmelaxme ,Rosarin Sruamsiri, Piyameth Dilokthornsakul, Teerapon Dhippayom Clinical effects of Zingiber cassumunar (Plai): A systematic review 35:30-77.

200. Wilawan Damkerngsuntorn, MD,1 Pawinee Rerknimitr, MD, MSc,1 Ratchathorn Panchaprateep, MD, PhD,1 Natsinee Tangkijngamvong, MD,1 Chanat Kumtornrut, MD, MSc,1 Stephen J. Kerr, PhD,2 Pravit Asawanonda, MD, DSc,1 Mayuree H. Tantisira, PhD,3 Phisit Khemawoot, PhD4,* The Effects of a Standardized Extract of Centella asiatica on Postlaser Resurfacing Wound Healing on the Face: A Split-Face, Double-Blind, Randomized, Placebo-Controlled Trial.`